AF412278

THE SOURCES FOR THE HISTORY OF THE COUNCIL

THE SOURCES FOR THE HISTORY OF THE COUNCIL

IN THE

SIXTEENTH & SEVENTEENTH CENTURIES

BY

E. R. ADAIR, M.A.

KENNIKAT PRESS
Port Washington, N. Y./London

THE SOURCES FOR THE HISTORY OF THE COUNCIL

First published in 1924
Reissued in 1971 by Kennikat Press
Library of Congress Catalog Card No: 70-118458
ISBN 0-8046-1206-4

Manufactured by Taylor Publishing Company   Dallas, Texas

PREFACE

Though the printed books and manuscripts cited
in this pamphlet appear to range over the whole field
of sixteenth and seventeenth century history, a very
definite attempt has been made to restrict the
references to works which are directly of value for
the history of the Privy Council during that period.
Hence, though at the first glance there may seem
to be certain arbitrary omissions, these can, I
think, be fully justified when it is remembered that
this is a strictly specialised bibliography, and not a
general one.

A more serious criticism can be based on the blight
of appendices that appears to have descended upon
this work, but their multiplicity seemed the only way
to avoid loading the text and the notes with an in-
sufferable number of references. The appendices,
also, are in each case merely detailed expansions
of a certain section in the text; they do not, if taken
together, form a bibliography of the subject, though
some care has been taken, by cross-references, to
render each appendix self-contained; consequently,
the subject-matter of each appendix has been dictated
solely by the needs of the text, and not by any pre-
conceived notion of a scientifically classified bibliography.

In order to make reference to the works that I
have cited as easy as possible, I have striven always
to give the exact title, the full initials of the author,
and the date of first publication, or of what I consider
the best edition if that is not the first one; the place
of publication has been given only in exceptional

cases. The titles of printed books and articles have been given in italics; those of manuscripts in ordinary roman type.

The dogmatism which the limits of space has imposed on the judgments I have expressed, the errors which such a bibliography cannot fail to contain, are my own; but whatever merit it may achieve must be shared with my wife, with Mr. H. W. V. Temperley, and with those of my colleagues and students who have, often all unknowingly, assisted me in its compilation. To them my thanks are due, as also they are to the Master and Fellows of Peterhouse, whose liberality first enabled me to embark upon the study of the constitutional history of the seventeenth century.

E. R. ADAIR.

April 26, 1923.

CONTENTS

	PAGE
PREFACE	iii
LIST OF ABBREVIATIONS	vi

SECTION

1. ORIGINAL SOURCES FOR PRIVY COUNCIL HISTORY	7
2. MODERN WORKS ON THE CONSTITUTIONAL POSITION OF PRIVY COUNCIL AND CABINET	34
3. BIOGRAPHIES	40
4. LEGAL AND COLONIAL ACTIVITIES OF THE PRIVY COUNCIL	41
5. ECONOMIC ACTIVITIES OF THE PRIVY COUNCIL	44
6. PRIVY COUNCIL AND LOCAL GOVERNMENT	45
7. PRIVY COUNCIL AND IRELAND	47
8. PRIVY COUNCIL AND ECCLESIASTICAL AFFAIRS	47
9. PRIVY COUNCIL AND FOREIGN AFFAIRS	48
10. PRIVY COUNCIL AND THE NAVY	49
11. SOCIAL ACTIVITIES OF THE PRIVY COUNCIL	50
12. PRIVY COUNCIL AND PARLIAMENT	51
13. STAR CHAMBER	53
14. COURT OF REQUESTS, COUNCIL OF THE NORTH, COUNCIL OF WALES, AND COUNCIL IN THE WEST	54

APPENDIX

I. BIBLIOGRAPHIES	56
II. III. } CONTEMPORARY COLLECTIONS OF MANUSCRIPTS	57, 64
IV. GENERAL MISCELLANEOUS COLLECTIONS OF MANUSCRIPTS	67
V. COLLECTIONS OF DIPLOMATIC CORRESPONDENCE FROM FOREIGN AMBASSADORS IN ENGLAND	71
VI. DIARIES, AUTOBIOGRAPHIES, MEMOIRS, CONTEMPORARY HISTORIES AND BIOGRAPHIES	78

CONTENTS

APPENDIX   PAGE

VII. CONTEMPORARY ACCOUNTS OF THE PRIVY COUNCIL, STAR CHAMBER, AND COURT OF REQUESTS - - - - - 81

VIII. MODERN WORKS ON THE CABINET AND CONDITIONS WITHIN THE COUNCIL - - 82

IX. NON-CONTEMPORARY BIOGRAPHIES - - 84

X. MISCELLANEOUS MONOGRAPHS - - - 86

XI. MODERN WORKS DEALING WITH THE RELATIONS BETWEEN PRIVY COUNCIL AND COLONIES - 88

XII. MODERN WORKS ON ECONOMIC HISTORY - 89

XIII. MANUSCRIPTS AND MODERN WORKS ILLUSTRATING THE PRIVY COUNCIL'S LOCAL ACTIVITIES 90

XIV. MODERN WORKS DEALING WITH THE PRIVY COUNCIL'S RELATION TO ECCLESIASTICAL AFFAIRS - - - - - 93

XV. MANUSCRIPTS AND MODERN WORKS VALUABLE FOR THE HISTORY OF THE STAR CHAMBER - 94

ABBREVIATIONS

Add. MSS.	.. Additional Manuscripts.
A.H.R.	.. *American Historical Review.*
B.M.	.. British Museum.
E.H.R.	.. *English Historical Review.*
Harl. MSS.	.. Harleian Manuscripts.
Hist. MSS. Com., 1st Rep., App.	*Historical Manuscripts Commission, 1st Report, Appendix.*
Lansd. MSS.	.. Lansdowne Manuscripts.
P.R.O.	.. Public Record Office.
Rep. of Dep. Keeper ..	.. *Report of Deputy Keeper of the Public Records.*
Ser.	.. Series.
S.P. Dom	.. State Papers, Domestic.
Trans. of the R. Hist. Soc.	.. *Transactions of the Royal Historical Society.*

THE SOURCES FOR THE HISTORY OF THE COUNCIL IN THE SIXTEENTH AND SEVENTEENTH CENTURIES

So wide were its interests, so all-embracing its activities, that the history of the Privy Council during the sixteenth and seventeenth centuries is really little less than a history of England during that period. Although there were many matters that were not referred to it, nothing was too great and nothing too small to be outside its competence; and if some questions of the first importance were kept from its consideration as a body, it was only because they were reserved for a small select group of its members on whom the Sovereign relied for secrecy and despatch.

The Privy Council was " the representative body of the King's Majesty," and even in the early seventeenth century few doubts had as yet assailed the King as to what he might do and what he might not. Consequently, the King in Council interpreted his duties and responsibilities towards his subjects in the very widest sense: his Council was there to give them relief when they felt aggrieved or, at least, to show them how such relief could be attained, to punish and to reward, to stimulate commerce, to inculcate industry, and to crush illegitimate discontent. Regulation was the almost unquestioned fetich of the age, and the Council was prepared to adjust in his own interests the smallest and most intimate details of a man's life. It safeguards youth by ordering that in all grammar and free schools the *Anglorum Prælia* in Latin verse by a certain Christopher Ockland shall be " publicly read and taught by schoolmasters unto their scholars " in place of " such lascivious, poets . . . from the which the youth of the realm receive rather infection in manners and education than advancement in virtue."[1] If the young man has deserved well, if " his towardliness and industry have not only advanced him to the Sixth Form " in his school, but have " made him capable and fit for the Seventh, which is the next step to be promoted to the University," then the Council will recommend his merits to his headmaster's eye.[2] It will see that he enjoys during his lifetime the privilege of using soap that is sweet and good and serviceable, and, if necessary, it will press its sale upon the justices of the peace[3] with a vigour equal to that with which it attacks the greatest affairs of state. And when he dies it will take care that his corpse is wrapt in good English woollen cloth, and not in foreign linens, whose sale does not benefit domestic prosperity.

Nor must it be thought that it was only its own ordinances or the royal letters patent that the Council enforced: without its stimulation, many of the most valuable of Parliament's enactments would have remained a dead letter; it was its constant supervision that kept the local executive active and efficient; it was the Council that saw to it that the Statute of Artificers or the Elizabethan Poor Law was carried into effect, and one of the most striking characteristics of the second half of the seventeenth

[1] J. R. Dasent: *Acts of the Privy Council*, vol. xiii., pp. 389-390, April 21, 1582.

[2] Privy Council Register, No. 42, p. 213, September 30, 1632 (the spelling has been modernised). This was the case of Master Cockes at Westminster School.

[3] S.P. Dom., Charles I., cclii. 21; ccliv. 34; cclx. 119. December, 1633 to February, 1634.

century is to be found in the comparative inertia of the Council in matters of domestic administration, and the chaos and abuse that resulted in the social and economic regulation of the country.

But in the midst of so much detail the Council never forgot that it was also its duty to advise the Crown on matters of high policy; sometimes, indeed, an inner circle of councillors might first be consulted, but in the majority of cases, before action was taken, the matter came before the Privy Council, and the discussions by that body were often by no means mere colourless justifications of decisions that had already been made; it was no accident that, of the two favourites of the earlier Stuarts, Somerset, the royal plaything before all else, rarely appeared at the Council table, while Buckingham, who aspired to be statesman and administrator as well, was a regular attendant. But here, again, the later seventeenth century saw a very definite dimming of the Council's lustre before the rising sun of the Foreign Committee, the Committee of Intelligence, the Cabinet, or whatever the inner circle of the moment might call itself.

It may therefore be said that the historian approaches the sources for the history of the Privy Council with a view to the examination of three great questions:

(a) What functions did it possess, and what powers did it exercise at different stages in its development, and by what process did it gradually rise throughout the sixteenth century to the zenith of its activity in the first half of the seventeenth ?— a rise due not only to its own increasing energy, but also to the appearance of that fuller appreciation of the government's responsibilities which was so marked during the sixteenth century, and which was ever threatening to overwhelm the Council with too many of the petty details of administration.

(*b*) What were its relations, both legal and actual, with other departments of the government, with the great officials, most of whom were themselves members of the Council, with the King and the royal household, with English ambassadors abroad and foreign ambassadors at home, with colonial officials, with subordinate councils, and, above all, with the machinery of local administration, such as it was ?

(*c*) What were the conditions which governed the deliberations of the Council: where and how did it meet, how were its proceedings recorded, what committees were established, what were its rules of debate, and, most important of all, how is one to solve the recurrent problem of the development of an inner circle of councillors to whom the most important matters of policy were first confided ?—a problem which involves the origin of the Privy Council from the ordinary Council, of the Cabinet from the Privy Council, as well as the creation of small and ever shifting groups of advisers, who are often only just raised above the level of the royal favourites of the moment.

First of all, it is natural to turn to the official records of the Council's proceedings,[1] the Privy Council Registers, which commence in August, 1540, and continue down to the present day; between 1540 and 1700 seventy-seven volumes survive—an extraordinarily complete series, for there are only five gaps in the sixteenth century, one in the seventeenth, and none at all later;[2] the whole of the

---

[1] See Appendix I. (p. 56) for a list of some useful bibliographies of sixteenth and seventeenth century history.

[2] The gaps are: July, 1543 to May, 1545; May, 1559 to May, 1570 (this is partially filled by a volume of rather fragmentary rough notes); June, 1582 to February, 1586; August, 1593 to October, 1595; April, 1599 to January, 1600; January, 1602 to May, 1613. A volume of extracts from the Registers between 1550 and 1610 (B.M. Add. MS. 11402) was compiled by Ralph Starkey in the seventeenth century, and includes a little from those Registers that have perished.

volumes for this period have now been transferred from the Privy Council Office to the Public Record Office.[1] Of the Privy Council Office itself there are two interesting modern accounts which describe fully its contents and the vicissitudes which the Register has undergone in the past: one is by Professor C. H. Firth in the *Appendix* (pp. 107-110, 209) to the *Second Report of the Royal Commission on Public Records* (1914); the other, by Professor C. M. Andrews and Miss F. G. Davenport, is to be found on pp. 170-187 of their *Guide to the MSS. Materials for the History of the United States to 1783 in the British Museum, in Minor London Archives, and in the Libraries of Oxford and Cambridge* (Carnegie Institute of Washington, 1908).[2]

A small part of the Register (from 1540 to 1542) was published by Sir Harris Nicolas in 1837.[3] From 1542 to 1604 it has been printed by J. R. Dasent in thirty-two volumes, and in 1921 its publication was resumed with a volume covering the two years 1613 and 1614.[4] The entries in the Register refer-

[1] The only exception to this is the Register from May, 1545 to January, 1547, which is in the British Museum (Add. MS. 5476).

[2] Both these accounts are, however, now out of date in regard to the number of volumes of the Privy Council Register that have been transferred to the Record Office. In the *Report on the State Paper Office* (*30th Report of the Dep. Keeper, App.*, p. 259, No. 303) there is a very vivid account of the condition in which Mr. Pownall, secretary to the Board of Trade, found the early seventeenth-century Registers, when he was searching for them about the middle of the eighteenth century. This is printed more fully in W. Knox: *Extra Official State Papers*, pp. 11-12 (1789).

[3] *Proceedings and Ordinances of the Privy Council of England*, vol. vii., ed. by Sir N. Harris Nicolas.

[4] *Acts of the Privy Council of England*, 1547–1604, 32 vols., ed. by J. R. Dasent (1890–1907); *Acts of the Privy Council of England*, 1613–1614 (1921). The volume for 1615 has been printed and is awaiting publication.

ring to colonial matters between 1613 and 1783 have been transcribed and published separately in five volumes by W. L. Grant and J. Munro.[1] Each of the volumes of the printed Register is equipped with a substantial introduction, and these introductions often contain valuable information as to the nature of the original Register and the functions and organisation of the Council, its committees and its officials,[2] though some of Dasent's judgments are rather hasty and dogmatic. There are also two articles by the present writer in the *English Historical Review* which discuss the manner in which the Register was compiled and the relation to one another of the rough and the fair copies of it.[3] For the Register, as it is preserved at the Public Record Office, does not consist of volumes all of the same nature; some of the sixteenth-century ones are merely the clerks' rough copies, and the fair copies, if they ever existed, are now lost. The others are fair copies, the rough versions of which can sometimes be found in collections of manuscripts at the British Museum and elsewhere in England. It is unlikely that these rough copies will add anything of material importance to the Register as we know it, but they certainly contain a fair number of entries

[1] *Acts of the Privy Council of England, Colonial Series, 1613–1783,* 6 vols., ed. by W. L. Grant and J. Munro (1909–1912). Vol. vi. consists of unbound papers found in the Privy Council Office, and has practically nothing earlier than 1700.

[2] *E.g.,* in the introductions to vols. i. and ii. of the *Acts of the Privy Council, Colonial Series,* there is a very valuable discussion of the committee system under the Restoration, and in the Addendum to vol. v. of the same series is a most useful list of Privy Councillors, as given in the Register between 1613 and 1783.

[3] E. R. Adair: *The Privy Council Registers. E.H.R.,* vol. xxx., pp. 698-704 (October, 1915). *The Rough Copies of the Privy Council Register. E.H.R.,* vol. xxxviii., pp. 410-422 (July, 1923).

which, for some reason or other, the clerk did not think it worth while to transcribe.[1]

There are two considerable periods during the sixteenth and seventeenth centuries from which no official records of the Privy Council could be expected to survive: the first forty years of the sixteenth century and the Interregnum. It is now almost certain that the Privy Council took its rise as a definite entity from within the body of the King's Council somewhere about 1538,[2] and it is extremely unlikely that any continuous record of the activities, either of the ordinary Council or of the Privy Council, was kept before the commencement of the Privy Council Register in 1540. There are, however, two interesting if very brief reports of the Council's proceedings surviving from this early period. One is the so-called Liber Intracionum,[3] and the other

---

[1] The following are the rough copies I have been able to discover: B.M. Add. MS. 26748 (November 12, 1553 to March 9, 1554), B.M. Lansd. MS. 238 (November 20, 1558 to April 30, 1559), B.M. Egerton MS. 2555 (April 2 to April 30, 1661), B.M. Add. MS. 37820 (August 9, 1661 to March 30, 1667), B.M. Stowe MS. 489 (September 2, 1661 to January 28, 1670). There are also numerous lists of agenda and rough notes of Council meetings made by Edward Nicholas to be found among the State Papers, Domestic, of Charles I. And even transcripts made in the seventeenth century can sometimes be useful—*e.g.*, B.M. Lansd. MS. 1162 is a transcript of the Register from April 16, 1581 to June 27, 1582, and supplies the dates and other marginal information of which the activities of a later binder deprived the orginal Register, and whose loss Dasent deplores. It is unfortunate that Dasent almost always ignores such aids to judicious editing as these parallel versions provide.

[2] The appearance of Thomas Derby in that year as " clerc of the p[ri]vy counsaile " is the first evidence that we have of their existence as an organised entity. This is discussed by the present writer in an article on *The First Clerk of the Privy Council* in the *Law Quarterly Review*, vol. xxxix., pp. 240-244 (April, 1923).

[3] B.M. Add. MS. 4521, art. 9.

a transcript made by Ralph Starkey of the Council's proceedings on four days in July, 1485.[1]

For the Interregnum, on the other hand, the records are extremely full, but they are records of the substitutes for the Privy Council, not of the Privy Council itself. The Day Books, Order Books, and Entry Books of the Committee of Both Kingdoms, and of its successor, the Derby House Committee, the Order Books, Letter Books, Warrant Books, etc., of the various Councils of State, are all listed in their chronological order in the *P. R. O. List, No.* 43,[2] and are fully calendared in the eighteen volumes of the *State Papers Domestic* that cover the period from 1644 to 1660, while the Journal of Richard Cromwell's Council (September 3, 1658 to March 22, 1659) is in the possession of the Marquis of Bath at Longleat,[3] and the Register of the proceedings of the Council of State from June 7 to October 20, 1659, is now in the Bodleian Library.[4]

But the formal official account of the proceedings of the Privy Council and its cognate bodies is, after all, often very unsatisfactory. At many meetings—and those usually of the greatest importance—no clerks were allowed to be present, and consequently no minutes of them appear in the Register; and even when the clerks were present, many of the orders which they were called upon to write were not considered of sufficient importance to be entered in the

---

[1] B.M. Harl. MS. 297, art. 1; it deals with July 10, 11, 14, and 16, 1485.

[2] *P.R.O. List, No.* 43, pp. 33, 26, 39-42 (this supersedes *List No.* 3). There is also a Letter Book of the Commissioners for Scotland in London, August, 1645 to October, 1646 (B.M. Add. MS. 37978). They were members of the Committee of Both Kingdoms, and their letters throw light on its activities.

[3] *Hist. MSS. Com.*, 3rd *Rep.*, *App.*, p. 198.

[4] MS. Rawlinson, A 134; neither of these is calendared among the S.P. Dom.

Council records. Moreover, the Register shows little or nothing of the discussions in the Council, the parties into which it was divided, or the inner groups which grew up in its midst.   For this, other sources of information must be sought.   There are a few scattered minute books of special committees; for example, among the Foreign Entry Books (176-180) at the Record Office are the minutes of the Committee for Foreign Affairs between 1668 and 1678, the rough notes for which, in Williamson's hand, are S. P. Dom., Charles II., ccclxvi; while Add. MS. 15643 in the British Museum contains the original minutes of the Committee of Intelligence from May, 1679 to February, 1681, together with some isolated notes of its proceedings in later years; the series of Secretaries' Letter Books is also of considerable value in throwing light on the Council's activities.[1] But undoubtedly the greatest possibilities of fruitful research lie in the vast mass of State Papers which have been gathered together in the Public Record Office.   For the reign of Henry VIII. these, together with a very large proportion of the other available material, not only in the Record Office, but elsewhere in England and abroad, have been calendared by J. S. Brewer and J. Gairdner in the *Letters and Papers, Foreign and Domestic, of the Reign of Henry VIII.* (21 vols., 1864–1920), while selected papers from the Record Office have been printed in full in the eleven volumes of the *State Papers of Henry VIII.* (1830–1852).   From 1547 onwards the *Calendars of State Papers Domestic*[2] are confined

[1] These are in the Record Office, and cover the years 1661–1703; they are Entry Books, vols. i., iii., iv., x., xvii., xxxi., xlii., xliii., lvi., lxii., lxiv., lxviii., xcvii.-ci. See *P.R.O. List, No.* 43, pp. 67-69.

[2] 1547–1603, 7 vols. (1856–1871); 1603–1625, 5 vols. (1857–1872); 1625–1649, 23 vols. (1858–1897); 1649–1660, 13 vols. (1875–1886); 1660–1681, 22 vols. (1860–1921); 1689–1696, 7 vols. (1896–1913).   The uncalendared docu-

to manuscripts in the Record Office; they now cover the whole period down to 1696, with the exception of the years 1682–1689. Similar papers relating to Ireland have been dealt with in two groups: those in the Record Office calendared down to 1670 in the twenty-four volumes of the *State Papers, Ireland*,[1] and the Carew Papers in the Lambeth Library extending from 1515 to 1624, and calendared in six volumes.[2] The corresponding calendars for Scottish affairs are those of the *State Papers relating to Scotland and Mary Queen of Scots*[3] and of the *Letters and Papers relating to the Borders*,[4] both compiled from manuscripts in the Record Office and elsewhere in England, together with the two volumes of *Hamilton Papers*,[5] the originals of which are now in the British Museum.

---

ments are listed along with the others in the *P.R.O. List No.* 43, pp. 49-51.

[1] 1509–1603, 11 vols. (1860–1912); 1603–1625, 5 vols. (1872–1880); 1625–1660, 4 vols. (1900–1903); 1660–1670, 4 vols. (1905–1911). From 1670 State Papers relating to Ireland are included in the *Calendars of State Papers, Domestic*. It should be noted that the five volumes for the reign of James I. calendar papers in the British Museum and in the Carew and Carte collections and elsewhere, as well as those in the Record Office. See the valuable introduction to the *Calendar of S.P., Ireland*, 1603–1606.

[2] *The Carew Papers*, 6 vols., ed. by J. S. Brewer and W. Bullen (1867–1873). These volumes must be used with great care, as the calendaring was rather carelessly carried out. Some very valuable letters from Cecil to Carew have been printed in full in *Letters from Sir Robert Cecil to Sir George Carew*, ed. by J. Maclean (Camden Soc., No. 88, 1864). There is also a valuable *Report on the Carte and Carew Papers* by T. D. Hardy and J. S. Brewer (1864).

[3] 9 vols., 1547–1588, ed. by J. Bain and W. K. Boyd (1898–1916).

[4] 2 vols., 1560–1603, ed. by J. Bain (1894–1895).

[5] 1532–1590, ed. by J. Bain (1890–1892). The originals are in the B.M. (Add. MSS. 32646-32657). The *Hamilton Papers* include some of the Sadler Papers (see App. I.).

These various collections of State Papers are all extremely miscellaneous in nature, and it is largely this fact that constitutes their value for the study of the history of the Privy Council; among them may be found orders of the Council or of its committees, reports of its deliberations, correspondence to which its orders have given rise, agenda for its meetings, accounts of the opinions of individual councillors from their friends, their enemies, or the more public if less reliable voice of court rumour as caught by the newswriter of the day. There is, in short, hardly one of the many problems that beset the study of the activities and composition of the Council upon which light cannot be thrown by an examination of these documents. But though these are the greatest, they are not the only collections of this type. Closely allied to them are the accumulations of letters and papers which were made by leading statesmen of the day, who were naturally also always members of the Privy Council; sometimes they kept copies of their own letters, very often they retained the orders which were addressed to them by the Privy Council and the letters that they received from fellow-members of the Council or from relations or dependents, reporting their own doings, and describing the course of current affairs; in many cases, too, if they occupied official positions, they retained in their own possession those documents which they had received in their official capacity.

Foremost among these must be mentioned the great collection of Cecil MSS. that is now housed partly at Hatfield House and partly at the British Museum. These manuscripts include a large portion of the papers not only of Lord Burghley and of his son, Robert Cecil, Earl of Salisbury, but also of the Earl of Essex and Sir Walter Raleigh; for the charge of high treason, for which they both suffered, naturally involved the confiscation of their papers into the hands of Robert Cecil, the secretary of state. While by far the greater part of these papers are still at Hatfield,[1] a considerable portion of those that belonged to Lord Burghley remained in the hands of his secretary, Michael Hickes; 122 volumes of these found their way into the Lansdowne MSS. in the British Museum,[2] and a few were bought by Sir Robert Harley and are now in the possession of the Marquis of Bath at Longleat.[3]

Of equal importance with the Cecil MSS. are those that once belonged to Edward Hyde, Earl of Clarendon, and are now in the Bodleian Library at Oxford; they are especially valuable for the history of the Privy Council and its committees during the reigns of Charles I. (from 1630) and Charles II.[4] They have been calendared down to 1657,[5] and a

[1] Calendared down to 1603 by the Hist. MSS. Com. (*Hatfield MSS.*, vols. i.-xiv.). Some of these manuscripts at Hatfield have been printed in full in *A Collection of State Papers relating to Affairs in the reigns of Henry VIII., Edward VI., Mary and Elizabeth*, vol. i. (1542–1570), ed. by S. Haynes (1740), and vol. ii. (1571–1596), ed. by W. Murdin (1759). There are, of course, many letters from Burghley and Salisbury to be found in the collections of State Papers already mentioned.

[2] Lansd. MSS. 1-122; a few of these Burghley papers have strayed to Add. MSS. 34727, 34729.

[3] *Hist. MSS. Com., Longleat MSS.*, vol. ii. These papers, as well as those among the Lansd. MSS., were at one time in the possession of John Strype, and some of them have been printed by him.

[4] The Clarendon State Papers do not end with the death of Clarendon; they contain valuable material as late as 1689.

[5] *Calendar of the Clarendon State Papers*, ed. by Ogle, Bliss, and Macray, 3 vols. (1872–1876). These volumes contain summaries of documents from 1523 to 1657, but there are comparatively few before 1634; the summaries in vols. ii. and iii. are much fuller than those in vol. i. This calendar has been completed, and may be consulted in manuscript at the Bodleian Library. There is also a list

selection from them has been printed in extenso in the three volumes of *Clarendon's State Papers.*[1] Many of these papers were used by Clarendon in the *History* and the *Life,* and some have been printed elsewhere; for the history of the Privy Council one of the most valuable publications of this nature is the *Notes which passed at Meetings of the Privy Council between Charles II. and the Earl of Clarendon,* 1660–1667, which W. D. Macray edited for the Roxburghe Club in 1896.[2]

Though the Clarendon State Papers are valuable for the reigns of Charles I. and Charles II., they have comparatively little to tell us of the Councils of the Interregnum, and that little is always to be discounted by the fact that Clarendon, an exile, had largely to rely on the words of spies and scandal-mongers. This gap is covered fairly adequately by the Thurloe Papers, also in the Bodleian Library,[3] a selection from which was published by Thomas Birch in seven volumes in 1742.[4] Thurloe's position, first as secretary of the Council of State and clerk to the Committee for Foreign Affairs (1652), and then as secretary of state both to Oliver and Richard

---

of all the volumes in the Clarendon State Papers, with their terminal dates, together with an account of their gradual acquisition by the Bodleian, in F. Madan: *A Summary Catalogue of Western MSS. in the Bodleian Library,* vol. iii., pp. 113-156. Madan also describes the contents of a fair number of other Clarendon MSS. that do not technically form part of the Clarendon State Papers. Some of these are very valuable.

[1] Published in 1767–1786.

[2] The original is in 2 vols. Bodleian: MSS. Clarendon, 100-101.

[3] MSS. Rawlinson, A 1-73. Four stray volumes are B.M. Add. MSS. 4156-4159.

[4] T. Birch: *A Collection of State Papers of John Thurloe, Esq.,* 1638–1660, 7 vols. (1742). These papers do not begin to get numerous before 1644, and they are of most value after 1649.

Cromwell, gave him unrivalled opportunities of amassing documents of value for the history of the various Councils of State.

Nor are the Cecils and Thurloe the only secretaries of state who preserved important collections of papers; even at the end of the seventeenth century it would be dangerous to say that secretaries of state always turned over all their official correspondence to the State Paper Office, though we find that quite early in the sixteenth century the Crown is anxious to secure, as soon as a secretary leaves office, as many as possible of his papers, both public and private. Consequently, for this and other reasons a considerable number of collections of documents that once belonged to secretaries of state are to be found among the State Papers Domestic. At the Record Office, for instance, are the bulk of Walsingham's papers,[1] almost all those of Sir Edward Conway, a large number of those that once belonged to Sir John Coke and Sir Edward Nicholas, most of Sir Francis Windebank's, and practically the whole of Sir Joseph Williamson's, even to his private note-books and diaries,[2] as well as others of less value for the history of the Privy Council. But both

[1] Walsingham's note-book, from 1583 to 1584, is B.M. Harl. MS. 6035; his Journal, now in the Record Office, has been edited by C. T. Martin for the Camden Soc. (*Camden Misc.*, vol. vi., 1870). It is of value for its notes of Privy Council meetings in 1573–1574. Sir Dudley Digges in *The Compleat Ambassador* (1655) prints a good deal of Walsingham's correspondence while he was ambassador in France (1570–1573), but the work is full of errors.

[2] Some of Williamson's correspondence in the Record Office is printed in W. D. Christie: *Letters addressed from London to Sir Joseph Williamson while plenipotentiary at the Congress at Cologne*, 1673–1674, 2 vols. (Camden Soc., New Ser., Nos. 8 and 9, 1874). These contain some very interesting references to the Privy Council and its committees. The many volumes of MSS. that Williamson gave to Queen's College, Oxford, are almost entirely heraldic in their interest, and are of no value for the Privy Council.

Coke and Nicholas also handed down very considerable collections of papers to their descendants, the Coke MSS.[1] being particularly valuable for the Privy Council's relations with naval affairs under James I. and Charles I., while the Nicholas MSS.[2] derive still greater importance from the fact that before he became secretary of state Nicholas was secretary to Buckingham for Admiralty and Cinque Ports business and a clerk of the Privy Council. Sir Ralph Winwood's papers among the Buccleuch MSS. at Montague House[3] are valuable for Privy Council intrigues during the reign of James I., though it is probably on foreign affairs that they cast most light; and the same collection includes the extremely valuable correspondence of that Charles, Duke of Shrewsbury,[4] who was secretary of state from 1694

[1] *Hist. MSS. Com.*, *12th Rep.*, *App. I. and II.*, *Cowper MSS.*, vols. i. and ii. These are very valuable down to 1642.

[2] Nicholas Correspondence, B.M. Add. MSS. 37816-37823; B.M. Egerton MSS. 2533-2562, 2584; this also includes some of the papers of John Nicholas, Sir Edward's son, who was clerk of the Privy Council later in the century. B.M. Add. MS. 4180 is a series of extracts by Birch of Edward Nicholas' lost letter books. Selections from this and from the Egerton MSS. have been printed by Sir G. F. Warner in the *Nicholas Papers* (Camden Soc., New Ser., Nos. 40, 50, 57, and 3rd Ser., No. 31, 1886–1920), but these do not begin till 1641. There are also some letters from Sir Edward Nicholas printed in the appendix to vol. ii. of Bray: *Memoirs of John Evelyn* (1818).

[3] *Hist. MSS. Com.*, *Buccleuch MSS. at Montague House*, vol. i., *The Winwood Papers*. With this should be read E. Sawyer: *Memorials of Affairs of State in the reigns of Queen Elizabeth and King James I.* (1599–1613), 3 vols. (1725), which prints in full many of the Winwood Papers at Montague House; these are not included in the Hist. MSS. Com.'s calendar, though the introduction to it gives some corrections that ought to be made in Sawyer's work.

[4] *Hist. MSS. Com.*, *Buccleuch MSS. at Montague House*, vol. ii., parts 1 and 2. Some of Shrewsbury's correspondence (from August, 1689 to October, 1707) has been printed by

to 1698, and whose notes of the meetings of the Committee of the Council during these years throw a little light on a very obscure stage in the development of the Cabinet. Of the other secretaries of state during the sixteenth and seventeenth centuries, only Henry Coventry and Daniel Finch, Earl of Nottingham,[1] have left papers of any great value for Privy Council history, but there are a considerable number of other members of the Council whose papers repay study. With the exception of the letters that remained in the hands of his secretary, John Packer,[1] Buckingham's correspondence is rather disappointing from the point of view of the Privy Council, but the manuscript collections of his contemporary, Sir Julius Cæsar, are of very considerable value.[2] Cæsar was a methodical lawyer of second-rate ability, but great perseverance, who often kept quite elaborate notes of the Council meetings at which he was present, and preserved a large number of the Council documents that passed through his hands. The printed corre-

---

W. Coxe in his *Private and Original Correspondence of Charles Talbot, Duke of Shrewsbury* (1821). The papers there printed are not reported on by the Hist. MSS. Com. The correspondence of James Vernon (secretary of state, 1697–1702), which forms part of the Shrewsbury correspondence, has been printed in part by G. P. R. James in the *Letters of James Vernon addressed to the Duke of Shrewsbury*, 3 vols. (1841); these also are valuable for notes of meetings of committees of the Privy Council. There is further correspondence of both Shrewsbury and Vernon in the Spencer MSS. (*Hist. MSS. Com., 2nd Rep., App.,* pp. 12-20).

[1] See Appendix II. (pp. 57-63) for details of these papers, as also for those of some of the other secretaries of state.

[2] Cæsar's papers are to be found in B.M. Add. MSS. 10038, 10113, 11405-6, 11574, 12496-12508, 14027, 34324, 36767, 38170; B.M. Lansd. MSS. 123-174. Add MSS. 12496, 34324, and Lansd. MS. 160 are especially useful.

spondence of Thomas Wentworth, Earl of Strafford,[1] is of some interest, and his papers at Wentworth Woodhouse ought to be a mine of information, but they still apparently remain quite inaccessible to the historical student.

For the second half of the seventeenth century— a very critical period in the constitutional history of the Council—the Shaftesbury MSS. at the Public Record Office[2] are a little disappointing, and the collections of his great rival, the Earl of Danby, are far more extensive and important. A certain proportion of his papers are still in the possession of the Duke of Leeds at Hornby Castle, but as these were calendared somewhat briefly by the Historical Manuscripts Commission,[3] it is difficult to estimate their value for the Privy Council. Fortunately, however, a very considerable collection of his papers has come to the British Museum from various sources,[4] and these contain much incidental in-

[1] W. Knowler: *The Earl of Strafford's Letters and Despatches* (1739).

[2] They are calendared in the 33*rd Rep. of the Deputy Keeper of Public Records, App.*, pp. 211-269. These are of some value for the Privy Council, but very little is to be gleaned from the manuscripts calendared in the supplementary reports (34*th Rep., App.*, pp. 307-315; 35*th Rep., App.*, pp. 188-191; 39*th Rep., App.*, pp. 567-568; 43*rd Rep., App.*, pp. 606-608). None of these documents seem to be included in the *Calendars of State Papers, Domestic*. Some of the Shaftesbury MSS. were printed by W. D. Christie in *Memoirs, Letters, and Speeches of Anthony Ashley Cooper, First Earl of Shaftesbury* (1859), but they are of little value.

[3] *Hist. MSS. Com.*, 11*th Rep., App. VII.*

[4] See B.M. Add. MSS. 28040-28054, 28071-28094. Add. MS. 38849B was reported on very fully by the Hist. MSS. Com. while it was in the possession of Mr. J. Eliot Hodgkin (15*th Rep., App. II.*, pp. 185-202); it contains part of the correspondence (some letters and some drafts of letters) between Danby and the Hon. Ralph Montague in 1678. Some of them were printed in *Copies and Extracts of some letters written to and from the Earl of Danby (now Duke of Leeds) in the years* 1676, 1677, *and* 1678 (1710). The attack

formation as to the part played by the Privy Council and by the King in the government of the country; they are of especial value in the history of the early development of Parliamentary parties and their relationship to the ministers of the Crown[1]—a history which is of prime importance in establishing the exact position held by the small bodies of privy councillors from which the Cabinet has developed. Equally important, though in a rather different way, is the enormous mass of papers collected by the first Duke of Ormonde. These manuscripts are now divided into two parts: one part is included in the Carte MSS. in the Bodleian at Oxford; this was catalogued in very general terms by T. D. Hardy and J. S. Brewer in 1864,[2] and much more fully by C. W. Russell and J. P. Prendergast in the series of *Deputy Keeper's Reports*.[3]   The other part of the

---

which Mr. Jeaffreson makes in his report on Mr. Hodgkin's MSS. on Danby's methods of editing is not wholly justified by the facts.   There is also a considerable body of Danby's correspondence in the *Lindsey MSS.* (*Hist. MSS. Com.*, 14*th Rep.*, *App. IX.*), but it seems of no very great value for the Privy Council.

[1] The Essex Papers are also very valuable in this connection.

[2] *Report upon the Carte and Carew Papers.*

[3] 29*th Rep. of Deputy Keeper of Public Records*, pp. vii-xii; 30*th Rep.*, *App.*, pp. 504-529; 32*nd Rep.*, *App. I.*, pp. 1-236. These deal with all the Carte Papers, which include other valuable documents besides those that belonged to the Duke of Ormonde.   There is a manuscript calendar of the Carte Papers in the Bodleian, and they are briefly catalogued in F. Madan's *Summary Catalogue*, vol. iii., pp. 113-156. Some of the Ormonde MSS. were printed in T. Carte's *Collection of Original Letters and Papers concerning the affairs of England from* 1641 *to* 1660, 2 vols. (1739), and many were used in the composition of his *An History of the Life of James, Duke of Ormonde*, 3 vols. (1735–1736), but neither of these is of very great importance for the history of the Privy Council.   There are at the Record Office fifty-seven bundles of transcripts from the Carte MSS.

Ormonde MSS. is at Kilkenny Castle, and has been
elaborately reported on in nine volumes by the
Historical Manuscripts Commission;[1] the most
valuable volumes of this calendar from the point of
view of the Privy Council are New Series, vols. iv.-
vii.   One of Ormonde's most devoted correspondents
was Sir Robert Southwell, many of whose letters
appear in the Ormonde MSS., and who also made
elaborate collections of his own which his position
as a clerk of the Privy Council renders especially
important, and which were added to by his son,
Edward Southwell, who followed his father in that
office.   These are at present in the British Museum.[2]
One other Council clerk stands out during these
two centuries as having accumulated material of
the greatest value for the study of the inner working
of the body whose proceedings he recorded: this is
Robert Beale, whose papers passed into the hands
of Sir Henry Yelverton, and are now possessed
by Lady Calthorpe; they have been rather briefly
reported on by the Historical Manuscripts Commission.[3]   This does not by any means exhaust the
list of members of the Privy Council whose papers
should be consulted by the student of Council
history: there are Sir Thomas Edmondes and
William Laud, Archbishop of Canterbury, the two
brothers, Henry and Lawrence Hyde, Essex, the

[1] *Hist. MSS. Com.*, *MSS. of the Marquis of Ormonde*,
2 vols. and Index vol., New Series, 7 vols.
[2] B.M. Add. MSS. 34329-34346, 34349-34350, 34353,
34358, 34773-34778, 35099, 35100, 35101, 35107, 38015,
38142-38157, 38536, 38847, 38861.   Of these Add. MSS.
34349, 34350, 35099, 35107, 38847, 38861, are especially
valuable for their notes on the Privy Council.   There is
also a good deal of Southwell correspondence in *Hist. MSS.
Com.*, *Egmont Papers*, vol. ii.
[3] *Hist. MSS. Com.*, *2nd Rep.*, *App.*, pp. 39-46.   Egerton
MSS. 1693, 1694, and Stowe MSS. 570, 571, are four of
Beale's volumes that have found their way to the British
Museum.

Lord-Lieutenant of Ireland, Temple, Sunderland, Halifax, and Robert Harley, though the last belongs rather to the early eighteenth than to the seventeenth century; while the correspondence and other papers of some of the monarchs of this period—Edward VI., William III., and Mary II., for example—can be used with great advantage as the result of the very intimate association of the King with the details of government.[1]

But the papers that members of the Privy Council left behind them are by no means the only private collections that will provide information as to the working of that body. Much that is purely incidental in character, though certainly none the less valuable for that reason, may be derived from collections of three other types. In the first place, there are the masses of papers accumulated by men who had no very close official connection with the Privy Council; sometimes, like Sir Walter Aston or Lord Feilding, Francis Parry or Matthew Prior, they have, while serving their country abroad as ambassadors, received interesting court news from their friends in England; and this might often bear almost the character of an official pronouncement, for it was long the duty of secretaries of state to keep ambassadors informed of the most striking political developments at home. Sometimes a minor public official like John Ellis or Sir William Clarke, or, what was much the same, a dependent of some great man, an Anthony Bacon, shining in the reflected importance of the Earl of Essex, would receive letters from other minor officials whose positions perhaps enabled them to penetrate for a brief distance the mysteries of the inner circle of court politics; country gentlemen like the Gawdys of Norfolk, the

[1] Information as to such of the papers of these and other members of the Privy Council as are relevant to this subject will be found in Appendix II. (pp. 57-63).

Manners family of Belvoir, or Sir Daniel Fleming
of Rydal Hall, were kept abreast of the political
situation in London by friends and relatives who
were often themselves in close touch with the great
affairs of state, or, if such were not available, by
paid newswriters, whose letters are by no means to
be despised, for, though they often represent only
the current opinion of the moment, sometimes they
are exceedingly well informed.[1]

Then, secondly, there are miscellaneous general
collections that include documents relating to the
sixteenth and seventeenth centuries. Various
motives have led to their accumulation. Sometimes
a collection has been made with the view to shedding
light on contemporary history; this desire produced
the eight volumes of John Rushworth's *Historical
Collections*,[2] and moved John Nalson to issue his
Impartial Collection of the Great Affairs of State[2]
in two volumes as a counterblast to Rushworth's
too favourable treatment of the Parliamentary
cause. Rushworth in particular reprints a number
of documents that are valuable for Privy Council
history, though in most cases it is better to go
straight to the original manuscript rather than rely
on an old printed version that may be inaccurate.
Sometimes the pure joy of collecting seems to have

[1] A list of the most useful of these minor private collections will be found in Appendix III. (pp. 64-67).

[2] J. Rushworth: *Historical Collections*, 1618–1648 (8 vols.,
1659–1701); J. Nalson: *An Impartial Collection of the Great
Affairs of State*, 1639–1649 (2 vols., 1682); Nalson is decidedly royalist in bias. Part of the original collection
made by Nalson for this work is in the Portland MSS.
(*Hist. MSS. Com., Portland MSS.*, vol. i.), and the rest is
in the Tanner MSS. in the Bodleian; the manuscript collection is more valuable for the Council of State than is the
printed work. Some of Nalson's MSS. were printed as
appendices to Z. Grey's *Impartial Examination of the Third
and Fourth Volumes of Mr. Daniel Neal's History of the
Puritans* (2 vols., 1737–1739).

been enough, as in the case of Sir John Cotton, whose vast mass of manuscripts is now in the British Museum.[1] Or, again, a man may have made such a collection with a view to expounding the importance of his family in the history of the time; this is the explanation of the mass of seventeenth-century papers gathered together by Roger North.[2] And then there are many later writers who collected documents or copies of them either as a basis for historical work or in order to publish them for their intrinsic interest. These are of value for our purpose, because they often render accessible manuscripts the originals of which are now in private hands.[3]

And, lastly, there are the collections of despatches sent home by foreign ambassadors resident in this country. One of their chief duties was to report on English political conditions, and therefore these despatches contain a very great amount of information as to the activities of the Privy Council, and especially as to the development of intrigues and parties within it, though, of course, they must always be used with great care, for they normally suffer from a foreigner's misunderstanding of English life and English names, and often consist of little more than a careful analysis of public rumour. These can be usually consulted in full in the respective foreign archives, and therefore I shall con-

---

[1] The Cotton MSS. are especially valuable in showing the great part the Privy Council played in the management of foreign affairs in the sixteenth century, and especially during the reign of Elizabeth; they are of little value for this purpose after 1610, and practically end with Cotton's death in 1631.

[2] His papers are B.M. Add. MSS. 32504-32552; much of value can be gained from them in regard to the beginnings of the Cabinet.

[3] In Appendix IV. (pp. 67-71) will be found a list of the more valuable of the miscellaneous general collections.

fine myself to indicating what can be done by the student who is unable to leave England.[1]

For this purpose the Public Record Office calendars of documents preserved in foreign archives and relating to England are of inestimable value. The Spanish archives have been dealt with in two series: one which started at 1485 and has now reached the commencement of Mary's reign with its eleventh volume, and the other which covers the reign of Queen Elizabeth in four volumes.[2] Unfortunately the work both of transcription and editing has not in the past been done very accurately or very completely, and a study of these calendars must be supplemented by reference to the great Spanish publication, the *Coleccion de documentos inéditos para la historia de España* of Navarrete,[3] and the Belgian one of Kervyn de Lettenhove, the *Relations politiques des Pays-Bas de l'Angleterre sous le règne de Philippe II*.[4] The other great series

[1] For a list of the more important sources of this nature see Appendix V. (pp. 71-77).

[2] *Letters, Despatches, and State Papers relating to the Negotiations between England and Spain*, ed. by G. A. Bergenroth, Don Pascual de Gayangos, M. A. S. Hume, and R. Tyler, vol. i., 1485–1509 (1862); vols. ii.-viii., 1509–1547 (1866–1904); vols. ix.-xi., 1547–1553 (1913–1916). *Letters and State Papers relating to English Affairs preserved principally in the Archives of Simancas*, ed. by M. A. S. Hume, vols. i.-iv. 1558–1603 (1892–1899). The Spanish transcripts deposited in the P.R.O. cover the first half of the seventeenth century, and contain many of Gondomar's despatches (there is a catalogue of these transcripts in the Literary Search Room at the P.R.O.), and Bergenroth's transcripts of papers at Simancas (mainly between 1521 and 1549) are in the B.M. (Add. MSS. 28572-28597), while Froude's (rather unreliable) are B.M. Add. MS. 26056, and S. R. Gardiner's (1603–1625) are B.M. Add. MSS. 31111, 31112.

[3] In 112 vols. (Madrid, 1842–1895).

[4] Kervyn de Lettenhove edited the first ten volumes (1882–1891); from the eleventh onwards the work was continued by M. Gilliodts van Severen. Most, but not all, of

of calendars deals with the Venetian archives, and covers the period down to 1639 in twenty-four volumes.[1] These calendars are valuable, not only for the despatches which they summarise, but also for the full reports they contain of the "Relations" which the Venetian ambassadors on their return home had to make to the Senate describing the country where they had been residing and its government. These "Relations" and others not yet calendared are printed in full in the original Italian in the *Relazioni degli stati europei letti al Senato dagli ambasciatori Veneti nel secolo decimosettino*.[2] There has also been issued by the Record Office one volume of the calendar of *State Papers relating to English Affairs in the Vatican Archives and Library*,[3] and one volume of the *State Papers and Manuscripts existing in the Archives and Collections*

---

the documents are printed in full, and those in Spanish are provided with a convenient French summary.

[1] *State Papers and MSS. relating to English Affairs existing in the Archives and Collections of Venice and other Libraries of Northern Italy*, vol. i., 1202–1509 (1864); vols ii.-v., 1509–1554 (1867–1873); vol. vi. (in 3 parts), 1555–1558 (1877–1884); vols. vii.-ix., 1558–1603 (1890–1898); vols. x.-xviii., 1603–1625 (1906–1912); vols. xix.-xxiv., 1625–1639 (1914–1923). The Record Office also has a long series of Venetian Transcripts, as well as a very valuable collection of Venetian MSS. bequeathed to it by Rawdon Brown; these latter are catalogued in the 46*th* *Report of the Deputy Keeper, App. II.*, pp. 337-381. There is also a *Report on the Documents in the Archives and Public Libraries of Venice*, by T. D. Hardy (1866).

[2] Ed. by N. Barozzi and G. Berchet, Venice (1856–1878). Some of the earlier Relations exist in print or in transcript in England, but the *Venetian Calendars* summarise them so fully that it is unnecessary to enumerate them.

[3] Ed. by J. M. Rigg (1917). It covers the years 1558-1571. There is also an extensive and valuable series of Roman Transcripts at the Record Office; these include many of the despatches of Panzani, Con, and Rossetti. There is a complete catalogue of these in the Literary Search Room at the P.R.O.

of Milan.[1]   Of the French ambassadors' despatches
no calendars have been published, but M. Armand
Baschet was employed for some years by the Record
Office in making transcripts of those that survive
in the Paris archives.   This series of transcripts
more nearly approaches completeness for the
seventeenth than for the sixteenth century; details
as to the periods that M. Baschet's work covers
can be found in the *Reports of the Deputy-Keeper of
the Public Records.*[2] He also prepared a Report on the
documents in French archives relating to British
history,[3] and an extensive, though not entirely complete, list of the French ambassadors in England
from 1509 to 1714, together with information in
each case as to the present locality of their original
correspondence.[4]   This forms the basis of two
pamphlets which appeared under the general
editorship of Professor C. H. Firth on the diplomatic
correspondence between France and England during
the periods 1603–1688 and 1689–1763 respectively;[5]

[1] Ed. by A. B. Hinds (1913).   It covers the years
1385–1618.
[2] *35th Rep.*, p. xiii; *40th Rep., App.*, pp. 555-557; *42nd
Rep., App.*, pp. 731-732; *43rd Rep., App.*, pp. 609-610;
44th Rep., App., pp. 647-648; *45th Rep., App.*, pp. 408-409;
46th Rep., App., pp. 129-130; *47th Rep., App.*, pp. 1-2.
There is a complete catalogue of these transcripts in the
Literary Search Room at the P.R.O.
[3] *36th Rep. of the Dep. Keeper, App. I.*, pp. 230-258.
[4] *37th Rep. of the Dep. Keeper, App. I.*, pp. 180-194;
39th Rep., App., pp. 573-826.
[5] *Notes on the Diplomatic Relations between England and
France*, 1603–1688, by C. H. Firth and S. C. Lomas (1906);
and *Notes on the Diplomatic Relations between England and
France*, 1689–1763, by L. G. Wickham-Legg (1909).   To the
same series J. F. Chance contributed *Notes on the Diplomatic
Relations of England and Germany*, 1689–1727 (1907), and
*Notes on the Diplomatic Relations of England with the
North of Europe*, 1689–1727 (1913); these are not so valuable
for the Privy Council.   There is about to appear a similar
list of diplomatic correspondence between England and

these give considerable but by no means exhaustive information as to the existence of originals, printed versions, or manuscript transcripts. Finally, a great number of miscellaneous selections from the despatches of foreign ambassadors resident in England during the reigns of Charles II. and James II. will be found in the work of the Marquise de Campana de Cavelli on *Les Derniers Stuarts à St. Germains en Laye*.[1]

Another source of information as to the history of the Privy Council in these two centuries is to be found in a variety of narrative accounts, which contemporaries drew up for their own gratification and that of posterity. Sometimes these rise to the level of histories of their own times, the greatest and most valuable of these being Clarendon's *True Historical Narrative of the Rebellion and Civil Wars in England*,[2] which should be studied in conjunction with the *Life of Edward, Earl of Clarendon*,[3] and with Professor C. H. Firth's articles in the *English Historical Review* on the relationship between these two works.[4] Only second to Clarendon in importance is Burnet's *History of My Own Time* (1660–1713).[5]

France during the reign of Elizabeth, edited by F. J. Weaver. A very useful list of *Materials for English Diplomatic History*, 1509–1783, *which are to be found in the reports of the Hist. MSS. Com. or among the MSS. in the British Museum* has been drawn up by Miss F. G. Davenport; it is printed in the 18*th Rep. of the Hist. MSS. Com., App. II.*, pp. 357–402.

[1] 2 vols. (1871).

[2] The best edition is in 6 vols., ed. by W. D. Macray (1888).

[3] There is, unfortunately, no good critical edition; the last one is that of 1857 in 2 vols.

[4] *E.H.R.*, vol. xix., pp. 26-54, 246-262, 464-483 (1904); see also the article on Clarendon in the *Dictionary of National Biography*, by Professor Firth, and an interesting essay on *Edward Hyde* by the same author; this has valuable bibliographical information as to Clarendon's writings.

[5] 1st ed. in 2 vols. (1724–1734); ed. by M. J. Routh in 6 vols. (1833); the reign of Charles II. only, ed. by O. Airy

Neither Clarendon nor Burnet can, of course, be implicitly relied upon, but, when they have been stripped of personal and party bias, and the defects of failing memory have been allowed for, there is left a mass of information on matters connected with the history of the Privy Council which is hardly to be surpassed by any other contemporary narrative authority.

Equally valuable, on occasion, with the contemporary history is the diary, the autobiography, and the contemporary biography. Narcissus Luttrell's *Brief Historical Relation of State Affairs*[1] may be a mere series of casual jottings based mainly on second-hand information or even on rumour, but it tells one a good deal that would not otherwise have been known. With the *Memoirs and Travels* of Sir John Reresby[2] or Bulstrode Whitelock's *Memorials of English Affairs*[3] one is on firmer ground, the latter being especially valuable for the Council of State during the Interregnum. Temple's *Memoirs*,[4] on the other hand, are singularly dis-

---

in 2 vols. (1897). With this should be read H. C. Foxcroft: *A Supplement to Burnet's History of My Own Time* (1902); C. H. Firth's introduction to Clarke and Foxcroft: *Life of Burnet* (1907), supplements Ranke's discussion of the value of Burnet's writings in the appendix to his *History of England principally in the Seventeenth Century* (English transl., 7 vols., 1875).

[1] From September, 1678 to April, 1714. 6 vols. (1857). The manuscript original is in All Souls' College, Oxford.

[2] 1673–1689. Issued in 1734. A fuller, but not a complete, edition by J. J. Cartwright in 1875. The original is in the British Museum.

[3] From 1625 to 1660, but it is not really at all full until 1640; 4 vols. (1853). These are largely extracted from the manuscript " Annals of his own Life " (B.M. Add. MSS. 37341-37347).

[4] Sir William Temple's *Memoirs*, Part III., in the 1720 edition of his *Works*, vol. i., pp. 331-359, and App., pp. 361-364.

appointing; beyond his too flattering description of his own share in the Privy Council scheme of 1679, there is little of interest on any subject but foreign affairs. Of contemporary biographies, two stand out head and shoulders above the rest in their value for Privy Council history: Roger North's *Life of the Right Hon. Francis North, Baron Guilford*,[1] and John Hacket's *Scrinia Reserata*,[2] which is really an intolerably verbose biography of John Williams, Lord Keeper of the Great Seal and Archbishop of York.

The last type of narrative source is the contemporary history of the Council, usually either legal or antiquarian in nature. This must be used with some care, for both lawyer and antiquary are too prone to dwell on the traditional rather than the actual state of affairs, too shortsighted to perceive the changes that were taking place at the moment they were writing. Coke in his *Fourth Institute*, Lambarde in the *Archeion*, Sir Thomas Smith in his *De Republica Anglorum*, even Sir Francis Bacon, in a more general way, in his famous essay *Of Counsel*, all give valuable if somewhat varying conceptions of the Privy Council's position and functions in the State.[3]

These are the main groups of original sources for the history of the Privy Council in the sixteenth and seventeenth centuries. But the wise student, before he turns his attention to the original sources, will have striven to make himself acquainted with the work that modern historians have done on this subject; wilful disregard of your predecessors' labours is not only bad manners, but also bad policy. Of the

---

[1] Ed. by A. Jessopp, 3 vols. (1890).

[2] Written about 1653, and published in 1693. For other sources for Privy Council history of this nature see Appendix VI. (pp. 78-80).

[3] For bibliographical details of these and other contemporary accounts of the Privy Council, see Appendix VII. (pp. 81-82).

great narrative histories of the sixteenth and seventeenth centuries Gardiner[1] and Ranke[2] are, for this purpose, infinitely superior to and infinitely more reliable than Froude[3] or Macaulay;[4] indeed, no one can have worked long in this field without realising the debt that history owes to these two great scholars. For the earlier sixteenth century Strype[5] and Burnet[6] are still valuable, especially in regard to the religious activities of the Privy Council, though more as a result of the original documents that they print than for the accuracy of their conclusions. Professor Cheyney is at present engaged on a history of the last fifteen years of Queen Elizabeth's reign,

[1] S. R. Gardiner: *History of England*, 1603–1642 (10 vols., 1883–1884); *History of the Great Civil War* (4 vols., 1893). *History of the Commonwealth and Protectorate* (4 vols., 1903); *The Last Years of the Protectorate*, by C. H. Firth (2 vols., 1909), is really the continuation of Gardiner's work.

[2] L. von Ranke: *A History of England principally in the Seventeenth Century* (English transl., 7 vols., 1875). Ranke is especially valuable for the documents he prints in his appendices.

[3] J. A. Froude: *History of England from the Fall of Wolsey to the Death of Elizabeth* (12 vols., 1856–1870).

[4] T. B. Macaulay: *The History of England from the Accession of James II.* (5 vols., 1849–1861).

[5] J. Strype: *Ecclesiastical Memorials relating chiefly to Religion and the Reformation of it . . . under King Henry VIII., King Edward VI., and Queen Mary I.* (7 vols., 1822); *Annals of the Reformation . . . during Queen Elizabeth's Happy Reign* (7 vols., 1824); *Lives of Matthew Parker* (3 vols., 1821), *John Whitgift* (3 vols., 1822), *Edmund Grindal* (1821); the *Memorials of Thomas Cranmer* (2 vols., 1812); all these are valuable for the Privy Council. His *Life of Sir Thomas Smith* (1820) and of *John Aylmer* (1821) are disappointing in this connection. There was published in 1828 an excellent index in two volumes to his collected works. Many of the MSS. Strype used are in the B.M. Harl. MSS. or B.M. Lansd. MSS., Part I., and as he was none too accurate in his transcription, it is always better to refer to the original manuscript, if it can be found.

[6] G. Burnet: *The History of the Reformation of the Church of England*, ed. by N. Pocock, 7 vols. (1865).

one volume of which has already appeared;[1] this contains a useful account of the Privy Council and the Star Chamber, and of their functions.　Mr. Inderwick has written a short legal study of the Interregnum[2] which is equally valuable on the Council of State.　On the purely constitutional side there is no good history of this period.　Hallam[3] on many points is quite obsolete and misleading; Hearn's *Government of England*[4] is good as far as it goes, but it smells a little of the mere textbook; *The King's Government*, by R. H. Gretton (1913) is a slight but suggestive work; and though Professor W. S. Holdsworth in his *History of English Law* (7 vols.)[5] has a section on the Privy Council and the Star Chamber, it is little more than a general sketch of their judicial functions.　Sir W. R. Anson in his *Law and Custom of the Constitution* (5th ed., 3 vols., 1922) is mainly concerned with the government organs of to-day, but he does give an account of the development of the Cabinet system; and J. R. Tanner prefaces the appropriate sections of his *Tudor Constitutional Documents*, 1485–1603 (1922), with short historical accounts of the Privy Council, the Star Chamber, the Court of Requests, and the Councils of the West, the North, and of Wales.[6]

But if the general constitutional history of this period has been rather neglected, as much cannot be said for the more specialised study of the Privy Council.　Most students will start their investigations with Sir Francis Palgrave's *Essay on the*

---

[1] E. P. Cheyney: *History of England from* 1588 *to* 1603 (1914).

[2] F. A. Inderwick: *The Interregnum* (1891).

[3] H. Hallam: *The Constitutional History of England from the Accession of Henry VIII. to the Death of George II.*, 2 vols. (1827).

[4] W. E. Hearn: *The Government of England* (1887).

[5] See p. 95 under Holdsworth.

[6] The documents illustrating these subjects (pp. 213-335) are very well selected.

Original Authority of the King's Council (1834), for, though this does not pretend to deal with anything later than the reign of Henry VII., its treatment of the subject is very suggestive. Palgrave was followed by Professor A. V. Dicey, whose *Privy Council* (1887) was never expanded beyond the limits of an able prize essay; the same may be said of Lord Eustace Percy's *Privy Council under the Tudors* (1908), though the narrower limits of the subject permitted him to develop it in greater detail. Professor J. F. Baldwin, in his work on the *King's Council in England during the Middle Ages* (1913), carries his account down to the end of Henry VIII.'s reign, but his treatment of the early sixteenth century lacks that mastery which he displayed in the earlier period. Both Karl Hornemann in *Das Privy Council von England zur Zeit der Königin Elisabeth* (Hanover, 1912) and Miss D. M. Gladish in *The Tudor Privy Council* (1915) give straightforward but decidedly pedestrian accounts of the subject, sometimes marred by rather serious errors;[1] while Professor A. F. Pollard's three articles on *Council, Star Chamber, and Privy Council under the Tudors* in the *English Historical Review*[2] are valuable for co-ordinating and clarifying previous knowledge on the relationship between these bodies, though the section on the Privy Council suffers rather from being compiled solely from printed sources.

The central problem of Privy Council history—the development of the Cabinet and its relationship to one or other of the committees of the Council—was hardly attacked at all before 1912, though there had been general histories of the Cabinet before

---

[1] There are two quite good articles descriptive of the Privy Council in the sixteenth century in the *Edinburgh Review* (vol. clxxv., p. 145) and the *Quarterly Review* (vol. clxxvii., p. 131).

[2] *E.H.R.*, vol. xxxvii., pp. 337-360, 516-539 (July and October, 1922); vol. xxxviii., pp. 42-60 (January, 1923).

that date.   W. M. Torrens had produced his *History of Cabinets* in two volumes as early as 1894, and Miss M. T. Blauvelt's *The Development of Cabinet Government in England* appeared in 1902; but for the seventeenth century these provide little more than a general sketch, the details of which have been greatly modified by later work.

As early as October, 1906, an article had appeared in the *English Historical Review* by E. I. Carlyle on the *Committees of Council under the Earlier Stuarts*,[1] and when W. L. Grant and J. Munro were editing the *Acts of the Privy Council, Colonial*, they incorporated in their introductions to vols. i. and ii.[2] valuable discussions of the committee system after the Restoration.   In April, 1912, Carlyle returned to the charge in his *Clarendon and the Privy Council*[3]—a discussion of the position of the Privy Council during the period 1660–1667.   In the same month, but in the *American Historical Review*, appeared Professor W. Notestein's article on the *Establishment of the Committee of Both Kingdoms*[4]— a committee in which Gardiner saw the first germ of the modern Cabinet; and six months later came H. W. V. Temperley's study of the *Inner and Outer Cabinet and Privy Council between 1679 and 1783*.[5]

---

[1] *E.H.R.*, vol. xxi., pp. 673-685.

[2] 1909–1910.   This should be read in conjunction with the review of vol. ii. by Professor C. M. Andrews in the *A.H.R.*, vol. xvi., pp. 119-121 (October, 1910).   Professor Andrews has also contributed to the investigation of the Council's committees, but his *British Committees, Commissions, and Councils of Trade and Plantations, 1622–1675* (1908), views the matter largely from the colonial angle, and his work will be dealt with later.

[3] *E.H.R.*, vol. xxvii., pp. 251-273.

[4] *A.H.R.*, vol. xvii., pp. 477-495 (April, 1912).

[5] *E.H.R.*, vol. xxvii., pp. 682-699 (October, 1912); this was followed by an appendix of *Documents illustrative of the Powers of the Privy Council in the Seventeenth Century* (*E.H.R.*, vol. xxviii., pp. 127-131, January, 1913).

In July, 1913, Professor E. R. Turner published the first of a series of very able articles[1] in which he attempted a detailed examination of the Cabinet and its predecessors in the seventeenth and eighteenth centuries—an examination which led him to some extent to disagree with the conclusions of Mr. Temperley and of Professor Wolfgang Michael, who had, in the same year, published an article on the origin of the Cabinet system in the *Zeitschrift für Politik*.[2] In January, 1914, Sir W. R. Anson entered the fray with a paper on the *Cabinet in the Seventeenth and Eighteenth Centuries;*[3] and in April, 1916, Mr. Temperley summed up the difference between Sir William Anson, Professor Turner, and himself in a brief but admirable article on the *Inner and Outer Cabinets in the Eighteenth Century*.[4] The result has been a great accession of knowledge in regard to the various committees of the Privy Council that might have given rise to the Cabinet, and to the internal organisation of the Cabinet itself; but throughout there has been rather a failure to indicate the stages in the parallel growth of some liaison between the executive and the legislature, of some idea of that responsibility of ministers to Parliament which has really become the essence of the Cabinet system. Something was done in a general way to remedy this defect in an extraordinarily suggestive article contributed by Professor G. B. Adams to the *American Historical Review* under the rather unpromising title of *Magna Carta and the Responsible Ministry*.[5]

[1] For details of these articles and for other contributions to this subject see Appendix VIII. (pp. 82-84).

[2] *Die Entstehung der Kabinettsregierung in England. Zeitschrift für Politik*, vol. vi., pp. 549-593 (1913).

[3] *E.H.R.*, vol. xxix., pp. 56-78 (January, 1914); this largely concerns the eighteenth century.

[4] *E.H.R.*, vol. xxxi., pp. 291-296 (April, 1916).

[5] *A.H.R.*, vol. xx., pp. 744-760 (July, 1915). For the

But it is not only in modern works that definitely set out to discuss the Privy Council or the Cabinet that one should look for valuable information on these topics. Biographers must necessarily, on occasion, have much to say as to the part that has been played in the government of the country by the man whose life they are striving to depict; biographies of the leading statesmen of the sixteenth and seventeenth centuries may, therefore, prove of very great value for the shifts and intrigues of court life, for that struggle to gain the royal ear, and so wield the royal power, which was one parent at least of the infant Cabinet system. For the Council in the early days of the sixteenth century, Professor A. F. Pollard's *Henry VIII*.[1] and his *England under Protector Somerset*[2] are of very considerable value; and Nicolas' *Life of William Davison*,[3] though old, is still useful for the Privy Council during the middle years of Queen Elizabeth's reign. Just as no one could study the history of the Council under James I. without the aid of Spedding's monumental *Life and Letters of Francis Bacon*,[4] so no complete account of the Council of State could be given without reference to Professor David Masson's *Life of John Milton*.[5] For the Restoration period the outstanding biography for this purpose is undoubtedly Miss H. C. Foxcroft's *Life and Letters of Sir George Savile, First Marquis of Halifax*,[6] though F. R. Harris' *Life of Edward Mountagu, First Earl of Sandwich*,[7] contains a good deal of useful information on the Committee of Trade and Plantations of 1668. Miss Violet Barbour's life of *Henry Bennet, Earl of Arlington*,[8] throws a considerable light upon court

---

relation between Privy Council and Parliament see below, pp. 51-53.

[1] Revised edition, 1905.　　　[2] 1900.　　　[3] 1823.
[4] 7 vols. (1861–1872).　　　[5] 7 vols. (1871–1894).
[6] 2 vols. (1898).　　　[7] 2 vols. (1912).　　　[8] 1913.

intrigues, but one cannot help feeling that there is still a good deal more to be done before Arlington's true position in the Council and the government of the country is fully revealed.[1]

Monographs on other subjects also occasionally give incidental references of value to the activities of the Council, but on the whole these are not of very great importance,[2] except in those cases in which they concern themselves directly with one or other of the more important aspects of the Council's work. Undoubtedly one of these aspects that merits most attention, and has probably received least, is to be found in the judicial work that the Council performed as the Privy Council, and not as the Star Chamber; for the sixteenth century this has been to some extent investigated by Miss E. F. White in a thesis she prepared on the " Jurisdiction of the Privy Council under the Tudors."[3] She also discusses the appellate jurisdiction of the Privy Council, such as it was at that time. This subject has been dealt with much more fully in connection with another aspect of the Council's labours—its relations with the colonies—an aspect which has naturally received most attention from American scholars. For this more specialised study certain additional original sources may be indicated. The *Acts of the Privy Council, Colonial*, have already been mentioned, and with them should be read the *Calendars of State Papers, Colonial*,[4] the first seven-

---

[1] See Appendix IX. (pp. 84-86) for a list of such biographies as are useful for the history of the Privy Council.

[2] See Appendix X. (pp. 86-87) for a list of the most useful of such monographs.

[3] This was submitted for the M.A. degree of the Univ. of London, and has never been published. A short note by Miss White on the *Privy Council and Private Suitors in* 1603, which appeared in the *E.H.R.*, vol. xxxiv., pp. 588-589 (October, 1919), is marred by the inaccuracy of its conclusions.

[4] Vols. i., 1574–1660 (1860); v., 1661–1668 (1880

teen volumes of which cover the sixteenth and seventeenth centuries. The manuscripts in the Public Record Office relating to the Lords of Trade and the Councils of Trade and Foreign Plantations have been indexed and described in Professor C. M. Andrews' *Guide to the Materials for American History to* 1783,[1] and are catalogued in the P.R.O. List, No. 36; and something has been done to blaze a path for the student through the wilderness of these records by C. S. S. Higham in his *Colonial Entry Books.*[2] The Plantation Books[3] are still at the Privy Council Office, but they have been adequately indexed by references given in the *Acts of the Privy Council, Colonial ;* the papers of Povey and Long[4] in the British Museum are of considerable value for colonial and trade regulation by the various committees and councils under Cromwell and Charles II. The complicated history of the various bodies which investigated trade and colonial questions and their relationship to the Privy Council or the Council of State has been very ably elucidated for the period 1622–1675 by Professor C. M. Andrews in his *British Committees, Commissions, and Councils of Trade and*

---

vii., 1669–1674 (1889); and ix.-xviii., 1675–1699 (1894–1908), deal with America and the West Indies.   Vols. ii.-iv., 1513-1624 (1862–1878); vi., 1625–1629 (1884); and viii., 1630–1634 (1892), deal with the East Indies, China, Japan, and Persia; this series is continued by W. Foster: *Court Minutes of the East India Company,* 1635 1663 (6 vols., 1907–1922).

[1] Carnegie Institution of Washington, 2 vols. (1912–1914).

[2] Helps for the Student of History, No. 45 (1921).

[3] Vol. i. runs from 1677 to 1700; it contains colonial laws approved by the Privy Council, instructions issued to governors, etc.

[4] B.M. Egerton MS. 2395, B.M. Add. MSS. 11410, 11411, 12429; Add. MSS. 12410, 12411, and 12423 are not very important.   Add. MS. 25115 contains interesting matter in regard to the Council of Trade of 1660.

Plantations.[1] The task was continued by Miss W. T. Root in her article in the *American Historical Review* on the *Lords of Trade and Plantations, 1675–1696*,[2] and brought to a conclusion so far as the seventeenth century is concerned by Miss M. P. Clarke, who, in the same periodical, described the *Board of Trade at Work*[3] from 1696 onwards. The whole matter has also been surveyed in a more general way by Professor C. M. Andrews himself in his volume on *Colonial Self-Government, 1652–1689*,[4] in the American Nation Series, and by H. L. Osgood in the third volume of his *American Colonies in the Seventeenth Century*;[5] while O. M. Dickerson, in his work on *American Colonial Government, 1696–1765*,[6] has an exceedingly useful study of the Board of Trade and the Privy Council at the close of the century. C. S. S. Higham—an English scholar, and almost the only one in this particular field— has attacked the earlier stages of this same problem from the point of view of the West Indies in *The Development of the Leeward Islands under the Restoration, 1660–1688*.[7] The rather specialised matter of the control of colonial legislation by the home government has been dealt with by E. B. Russell in the Columbia University Studies under the title of *The Review of American Colonial Legislation by the King in Council*,[8] while the question of the Privy

---

[1] Johns Hopkins Univ. Studies in History and Political Science, vol. xxvi. (1908).

[2] *A.H.R.*, vol. xxiii., pp. 20-41 (October, 1917).

[3] *A.H.R.*, vol. xvii., pp. 17-43 (October, 1911).

[4] 1904. Chap. II. (English Administration of the Colonies, 1651–1672) is especially good, and there is a good critical bibliography.　　　　　　[5] 3 vols. (1904–1907).

[6] 1912. This also has an excellent bibliography.

[7] 1921. Chap. IX. is the most valuable one for this purpose; there is quite a useful bibliography.

[8] Columbia Univ. Studies in History, Economics, and Public Law, vol. lxiv., No. 2 (1915). Chap. I. deals with the subject down to 1696.

Council's appellate jurisdiction is discussed by A. M. Schlesinger in two valuable articles in the *Political Science Quarterly* for 1913.[1] Finally, the two works of G. L. Beer, which are concerned with the sixteenth and seventeenth centuries—*The Origins of the British Colonial System, 1578–1660*,[2] and *The Old Colonial System*[3]—not only deal ably with the Committees of Plantations and Trade, but also form one of the most valuable monographs on another aspect of the Privy Council's activity—its control of economic conditions at home and in the colonies.

This subject has, indeed, received very insufficient attention, and there is no single account of the Privy Council's multifarious labours in the economic sphere; the better type of textbook—Cunningham's *Growth of English Industry and Commerce*,[4] for example—certainly notes, on occasion, the guiding hand of the Privy Council, though without emphasising sufficiently its supreme importance in the century which passed between 1550 and 1650. More specialised monographs also afford examples of the Privy Council's universal competence; in industry, Professor G. Unwin in his *Industrial Organisation in the Sixteenth and Seventeenth Centuries*[5] repeatedly calls attention to the Privy Council's control over the gilds. Miss E. M. Leonard in *The Early History of the English Poor Relief*[6] rightly emphasises the fact that it was the eye of the Privy Council that supervised the whole system, while Dr. W. R. Scott

---

[1] *Colonial Appeals to the Privy Council.*   *Political Science Quarterly*, vol. xxviii., pp. 279, 433 (1913).

[2] 1908.

[3] Only Part I.—*The Establishment of the System, 1660–1688* (2 vols., 1912)—has been published.   For other works dealing with the Privy Council's relations with the colonies see Appendix XI. (pp. 88-89).

[4] 3 vols. (1905–1907).

[5] 1904.   [6] 1900.

in his encyclopædic *Constitution and Finance of English, Scottish, and Irish Joint Stock Companies to 1720*[1] supplies a great deal of evidence of the Privy Council's care for trade and its regulation.

A subject that can hardly be dissociated from the economic aspect of the Privy Council's activities is that of its relationship with the officials of the local government and with matters of local interest. This can be traced with considerable profit in municipal records, in the manuscript Repertories and Journals at the London Guildhall,[2] for example, or in the manuscripts of the City of Exeter,[3] or of the Corporations of Rye,[4] of Plymouth,[5] or of Chester,[6] to name but four of those calendared by the Historical Manuscripts Commission; almost

---

[1] 3 vols. (1910–1912). See Appendix XII. (pp. 89-90) for a list of other modern works dealing with economic history that are valuable for that of the Privy Council.

[2] W. H. and H. C. Overall, in their *Analytical Index to the Series of Records known as the Remembrancia*, 1579–1664 (1878), calendar many documents which indicate the extent of the Privy Council's correspondence with the London government.

[3] *Hist. MSS. Com., MSS. of the City of Exeter* (1916). Especially interesting is the Privy Council's intervention in the great struggle between William Perryman, schoolmaster of the High School, and the City of Exeter (1622–1630).

[4] *Hist. MSS. Com., 13th Rep., App. IV.* These illustrate the great care taken by the Privy Council to supervise the movements of Englishmen and foreigners either into or out of England.

[5] *Hist. MSS. Com., 9th Rep., App.,* pp. 262-284. The two volumes known as the Woolcumbe Folios (pp. 263-272) are especially valuable.

[6] *Hist. MSS. Com., 8th Rep., App., Pt. I.,* pp. 373-400. These show the Privy Council much concerned with the transport of soldiers from Chester to Ireland. B.M. Harl. MS. 2091 and B.M. Stowe MS. 812 contain the papers concerning the great dispute over tolls between Chester and Sir Ranulph Crewe (1627–1631), and show the Privy Council's interference in the matter.

invariably these show a steadily growing interest on the part of the Privy Council in the affairs of the borough during the later sixteenth and early seventeenth centuries, and its almost complete cessation after the Restoration.   The Quarter Sessions records in the counties are much more disappointing, as they indicate little more than a very occasional reminder by the Privy Council of the needs of a maimed soldier or of some such matter of mere routine; it is probable that the activity was there, but that it was not recorded, and there is plenty of other evidence of the way in which the Privy Council acted through the local justice of the peace, the sheriff and the deputy, or the lord-lieutenant of the county.   Sir Walter Covert as High Sheriff, Deputy-Lieutenant, and Justice of the Peace for Sussex, kept careful copies of the letters he received from the Privy Council, and these are now in the British Museum;[1] while among the manuscripts of Mr. E. R. Wode-house[2] are two letter books of the Deputy-Lieu-tenants and Justices of the Peace for the county of Suffolk; both of these collections may serve to illustrate the large part played by the Privy Council in local affairs.   This is further expounded in C. A. Beard's valuable monograph on the *Office of Justice of the Peace in England*,[3] while W. Rye in his *State Papers relating to Musters, Beacons, Ship-money, etc., in Norfolk from* 1626 *to* 1637[4] prints many documents

---

[1] Harl. MS. 703.   There is another collection of similar letters for Sussex (1583–1627) in Lord Leconfield's MSS. (*Hist. MSS. Com.*, *6th Rep.*, *App.*, p. 312); *cf.* also the Loseley MSS. (*Hist. MSS. Com.*, *7th Rep.*, *App.*, *Pt. I.*).

[2] *Hist. MSS. Com.*, *13th Rep.*, *App. IV.*, pp. 419–420, 433-469.

[3] Columbia Univ. Studies in History, Economics, and Political Science, vol. xx., No. 1 (1904).

[4] 1907.   There is a good introduction by Professor C. H. Firth.   See Appendix XIII. (pp. 90-93) for a list of MSS. and books on the local activities of the Privy Council.

showing the same activity in the more specialised aspects of local defence and local assessment of taxation.

Ireland enjoyed an even greater share of the Privy Council's attention, for Ireland was looked upon as being in a very special way dependent upon the care of the King and Council. The value of the State Papers, Irish, and the Carte, Ormonde, and Carew Papers in this connection has already been mentioned, and there are one or two other manuscript sources which might be consulted with advantage.[1] R. Bagwell's works on *Ireland under the Tudors*[2] and *Ireland under the Stuarts*[3] give what is probably the best account of the relations between the English and the Irish governments during this period, and for the Interregnum this can be supplemented by a study of the documents printed in R. Dunlop's *Ireland under the Commonwealth*.[4]

There are still several other aspects of the Privy Council's work which should claim the student's attention. To religious problems and the enforcement of the royal views in doctrine and in ceremonial observance the Privy Council naturally devoted a very considerable portion of its time, though its labours were greatly lightened by the existence of the Court of High Commission. The works of Strype and Burnet have already been mentioned; to these may be added the general *History of the Church of England*,[5] by R. W. Dixon, and the very much shorter and, for this purpose, more valuable

---

[1] *E.g.*, B.M. Add. MSS. 34773-34778, which contain many of the papers of Robert and Edward Southwell concerning Ireland (1686-1741); MS. Rawlinson A 149 in the Bodleian contains abstracts of letters from the King and Privy Council to the Privy Council in Ireland (1603-1609), and Lord Leconfield's MSS. contain a considerable amount of material as to the Privy Council's activity in Irish affairs between 1660 and 1666 (*Hist. MSS. Com.*, 6th Rep., App., pp. 316-318).

[2] 3 vols. (1885-1890).   [3] 3 vols. (1909).

[4] 2 vols. (1913).   [5] 1529-1570. 6 vols. (1877-1902 .

work by W. H. Frere.[1] Neal's *History of the Puritans*,[2] which covers practically the whole period, is also of some importance for the attitude of the government towards the Nonconformists. A special side of the subject—the activity of the Council in suppressing illegitimate pamphlets—is ably dealt with by W. Pierce in his *Historical Introduction to the Marprelate Tracts*.[3] A considerable number of valuable documents have been printed in the *Correspondence of Matthew Parker*[4] and in the *Seconde Parte of a Register*,[5] and many of these illuminate the attitude of the Privy Council in religious matters during the second half of the sixteenth century. F. Makower's *The Constitutional History and the Constitution of the Church of England*[6] is very disappointing as to the position of the Privy Council in relation to Church government.[7]

To foreign affairs, also, the Privy Council gave much of their attention, for the control of foreign affairs was the King's special prerogative. Almost any article on foreign policy or any collection of English or foreign ambassador's despatches will bear witness to this, but there has been very little written that deals specifically with the Privy Council's activities in this direction. Professor E. R. Turner touches upon the subject in his article on *Parliament and Foreign Affairs*, 1603–1760,[8] and V. Alexandrenko discusses the matter, so far as

---

[1] *The History of the English Church*, 1558–1625 (1904).

[2] D. Neal: *History of the Puritans*, 1517–1688, ed. by J. Toulmin in 5 vols. (1793–1797). It was first printed in 1732–1738.   [3] 1908.

[4] Ed. by J. Bruce and T. T. Perowne (Parker Soc., 1853).

[5] Ed. by A. Peel (1915); this is a calendar of documents or copies of documents collected by the Puritans about 1593 for publication.   [6] English transl. 1895.

[7] See Appendix XIV. (pp. 93-94) for a list of books on this subject.

[8] *E.H.R.*, vol. xxxiv., pp. 172-197 (April, 1919).

relations with Russia are concerned, in his contribution to the *Journal of the Minister of Public Instruction in Russia.*[1]

Equally important in the Privy Council's eyes was the control of the details of naval policy, and here it often acted through the Lord High Admiral—one of its own members—or the Admiralty Commission, though it never hesitated to communicate direct with the relevant official, if it desired so to do. Therefore, the first special source to which a student should go for evidence of this activity is the Admiralty records at the Public Record Office.[2] Naval administration during this period has been described by M. Oppenheim[3] and J. R. Tanner[4] in their various works, and Mr. Oppenheim in particular throws light on the position of

[1] *The Part taken by the English Privy Council in the Diplomatic Relations between England and Russia,* 1556–1649; *Zhurnal Ministerstva Narodnago Prosvestcheniya* (December, 1889). I have not had an opportunity of reading this. The *Calendar of State Papers, Foreign,* 22 vols., 1547–1586 (1861–1921), contains a great deal that illustrates the Privy Council's share in the control of foreign policy and their relations with the English ambassadors abroad.

[2] See *P.R.O. List, No.* 18, and an article by R. G. Marsden on the *High Court of Admiralty,* 1550–1650, in the *Trans. of the R. Hist. Soc.,* New Ser., vol. xvi., pp. 69-96 (1902). The papers of the Commissioners of the Navy are calendared among the State Papers, Domestic down to June, 1673. The Sandwich Papers form part of the Carte MSS. in the Bodleian, and as they are largely the papers of Sir Edward Montagu, they contain much in regard to Admiralty administration. The Coke MSS., the Nicholas MSS., and the Pepys MSS. are also valuable (see pp. 21, 66).

[3] *The Administration of the Royal Navy,* 1509–1660 (1896). This supersedes Mr. Oppenheim's articles in the *E.H.R.* for 1891–1894, 1896.

[4] His introductions on this subject to the volumes of the *Catalogue of the Pepysian MSS.* (4 vols., Navy Records Soc., 1903–1923) supersede his articles in the *E.H.R.* for 1897–1899. His lecture on *Samuel Pepys and the Royal Navy* (1920) is also interesting in this connection.

the Privy Council and the work that it did for the navy, while S. R. Gardiner and C. T. Atkinson, in their *Letters and Papers relating to the First Dutch War*,[1] have printed in full innumerable orders of the Council of State and the Admiralty Committees and Commissions during the years 1652–1654. There have also been written two interesting articles, one by Professor E. P. Cheyney on *International Law under Elizabeth*,[2] and the other by L. Abrahams on *Two Jews before the Privy Council*,[3] both of which deal with the Council's intervention in Admiralty law.

Finally, there is that rather miscellaneous aspect of the Privy Council's activities which was predominantly social in its nature. To the regulation of the theatre, for example, the Council gave a very considerable amount of care. Miss V. C. Gildersleeve in her *Government Regulation of the Elizabethan Drama*,[4] and T. S. Graves in the *Political Use of the Stage during the Reign of James I.*,[5] both discuss this matter at some length, while in the *Loseley Manuscripts*[6] are printed a large number of Privy Council orders connected with the Lord of Misrule under Edward VI.; for the early Stuarts Mr. E. K. Chambers has printed in the *Malone Society's Collections* all such portions of the Privy Council Register as refer to playwrights or the stage.[7]   The Post Office,

[1] 5 vols.   Navy Records Soc. (1898–1911).   J. R. Tanner prints the Admiralty Journal from 1674 to 1679 in vol. iv. of the *Catalogue of the Pepysian MSS.* (1923); this is valuable for the Council's naval activities during that period.

[2] *E.H.R.*, vol. xx., pp. 659–672 (1905).

[3] *Jewish Quarterly Review*, vol. xiv., p. 354 (January, 1902).

[4] Columbia Univ. Studies in English (1908); there is a good bibliography.   With this should be studied E. K. Chambers: *Notes on the History of the Revels Office under the Tudors* (1906).

[5] *Anglia*, vol. xxxviii., pp. 137-156 (1914).

[6] Ed. by A. J. Kempe (1835).

[7] E. K. Chambers and W. W. Greg: *Dramatic Records from the Privy Council Register*, 1603–1642 (1911).   *The Malone Society's Collections*, Pts. IV. and V., pp. 370-395.

also, was kept under careful control—a control which has been described both by J. C. Hemmeon in his thesis on the *History of the British Post Office*[1] and by J. W. Hyde in his older work on the *Post in Grant and Farm;*[2] the latter deals more especially with the seventeenth century. Professor E. R. Turner touches on the same matter in his article on the *Secrecy of the Post.*[3] Education also received its meed of attention, but in this direction the only reliable account is to be found in Professor Foster Watson's *The State and Education during the Commonwealth,*[4] and this covers but a very short portion of the whole period.

No study of the sources of the history of the Privy Council during the sixteenth and seventeenth centuries would be complete if some mention were not made of two other problems which a student might profitably investigate: the influence which the individual Privy Councillor exercised in Parliament by virtue of his Privy Councillorship, and the relations between the Council and the Star Chamber, the Council of the North, and other similar ancillary bodies.

In regard to the first matter, the prime sources of information will naturally be the *Journals* of the House of Commons and of the House of Lords,[5] supplemented on the one hand by the two Parliamentary Histories—Cobbett's,[6] which covers the period in five volumes, and the *Old Parliamentary History,*[7] which takes twenty-one volumes over the

[1] Harvard Economic Studies, vol. vii. (1912).

[2] 1894.

[3] *E.H.R.*, vol. xxxiii., pp. 320-327 (July, 1918).

[4] *E.H.R.*, vol. xv., pp. 58-72 (January, 1900).

[5] *Journals of the House of Commons*, 1547–1702, 13 vols. (1803); *Journals of the House of Lords*, 1509–1701, 16 vols.

[6] W. Cobbett: *Parliamentary History of England*, 36 vols. (1806–1820); vol. i., 1066–1625; vols. ii.-v., 1625–1702.

[7] *The Parliamentary or Constitutional History of England*, 24 vols. (1751–1761); vols. iii. and iv. 1509–1603; vols.

140 years between 1509 and 1660—and, on the other, by private reports of the debates. For the reign of Elizabeth undoubtedly the most valuable of these is the collection made by Sir Simonds D'Ewes;[1] this was largely compiled from the official journals of the Lords and Commons, some of which are now missing. For the seventeenth century, and especially for the first half of it, the number of privately kept journals of the proceedings in the House of Commons is too great to permit a list of them to be given here; but a useful bibliography of them will be found in J. T. Gerould's *Sources of English History of the Seventeenth Century in the University of Minnesota Library;*[2] the private journals for the sessions of 1628 and 1629 are very adequately described in Miss F. H. Relf's *Petition of Right,*[3] and W. Notestein's and Miss Relf's *The Commons' Debates for 1629*[4] respectively. For the post-Restoration Parliaments the most valuable private journal is Anchitell Grey's *Debates,*[5] which run from 1667 to 1694, and add a very great deal to our knowledge of the relations between the Privy Council or its committees and the House of Commons. The allied subject of the issue of writs of assistance to Privy Councillors has been

---

v.-xxiii., 1603–1660. This was one of the main sources for Cobbett's *Parliamentary History,* and they must both be used with great care, as they are very inaccurate and uncritical.

[1] *A Compleat Journal of the Votes, Speeches, and Debates, both of the House of Lords and House of Commons throughout the whole reign of Queen Elizabeth* (1682). J. E. Neale's article on the *Authorship of Townshend's " Historical Collections "* (*E.H.R.,* vol. xxxvi., pp. 96-99, January, 1921) shows how largely they are derived from D'Ewes' *Journal.*

[2] Research Publications of the Univ. of Minnesota, Bibliographical Series, No. 1 (1921), pp. 21-26.

[3] The Univ. of Minnesota, Studies in the Social Sciences, No. 8 (1917).

[4] The Univ. of Minnesota, Studies in the Social Sciences, No. 10 (1921).

[5] 10 vols. (1769).

discussed by the present writer and Miss F. M.G. Evans in the *English Historical Review*.[1]

Of contemporary accounts of those Councils which were in more or less close relationship to the Privy Council, a list has already been given.[2]   Of these various bodies, the Council in the Star Chamber was by far the most intimately associated with the Privy Council; it represented the judicial aspect of that same King's Council from which the Privy Council itself had sprung, and during the latter half of its existence it was in practice nothing more than the Privy Council afforced by certain judges and sitting in public to hear judicial causes.   The first modern critical study of the early Star Chamber was made by Miss C. L. Scofield,[3] but her work has, to some considerable extent, been superseded by I. S. Leadam in his introductions to the two volumes of the *Select Cases in the Star Chamber*,[4] by Professor E. P. Cheyney in the *American Historical Review*,[5] and, especially as to the early development of the Star Chamber, by Professor A. F. Pollard in his recent articles in the *English Historical Review*.[6] There are a very considerable number of manuscript collections of reports of cases in the Star Chamber in the British Museum and among the documents calendared by the Historical Manuscripts Commis-

[1] E. R. Adair and F. M. G. Evans: *Writs of Assistance.* *E.H.R.*, vol. xxxvi., pp. 356-372 (July, 1921).

[2] See Appendix VII. (pp. 81-82).

[3] *A Study of the Court of Star Chamber* (1900).   This has a good bibliography, especially of manuscript reports of Star Chamber cases in the British Museum.

[4] Selden Soc., vols. xvi. and xxv. (1902, 1910).

[5] *The Court of Star Chamber.*   *A.H.R.*, vol. xviii., pp. 727-750 (July, 1913).   There is also a good summary of the whole question in Professor Cheyney's *History of England from 1588 to 1603* (1914).

[6] *E.H.R.*, vol. xxxvii., pp. 337-360, 516-539 (July and October, 1922); vol. xxxviii., pp. 42-60 (January, 1923).

sion.   Many are printed in Hudson[1] and Haward;[1] Leadam collects others together in the *Select Cases in the Star Chamber*[2] which gives the more interesting ones between 1477 and 1544; and those in the Public Record Office are catalogued down to 1558 in the *List of Proceedings in the Court of Star Chamber ;*[3] in addition, certain local societies have printed the cases referring to their own counties.   There have also survived some very interesting accounts for the dinners which the Council consumed every week in the Star Chamber at the Crown's expense.[4]

For the Court of Requests part of the original sources in the Public Record Office have been catalogued in the *List of Proceedings in the Court of Requests,*[5] and I. S. Leadam has edited for the Selden Society a volume of *Select Cases in the Court of Requests,*[6] the introduction to which contains a valuable account of the origin and procedure of this body.

Miss R. R. Reid's work on the *King's Council of the North* (1921) deals exhaustively with this subject, and to this the student is referred for further bibliographical information.   Of the two remaining Councils—those of Wales and of the West—Miss C. A. J. Skeel has in each case written the standard account.   The short-lived Council of the West she dealt with in the *Transactions of the Royal Historical*

---

[1] See Appendix VII., pp. 81, 82.   [2] See p. 53.

[3] *P.R.O. List, No.* 13 (1901).   This supersedes the 49*th Rep. of the Dep. Keeper of Public Records, App.*, pp. 376-594. See also M. S. Giuseppi: *A Guide to the Manuscripts preserved in the Public Record Office*, vol. i., pp. 272-273 (1923).

[4] For these and other works bearing on the Star Chamber see Appendix XV. (pp. 94-96).

[5] *P.R.O. List, No.* 21 (1906).   This goes down to the end of Philip and Mary's reign, and includes a few cases from the early years of Elizabeth.   See also Giuseppi's *Guide,* vol. i., pp. 270-271.

[6] 1898.   This runs from 1497 to 1569.   See also Appendix VII. (pp. 81-82).

Society for 1921,[1] and her work on the *Council in the Marches of Wales*,[2] if read in conjunction with her supplementary articles on the *Council of the Marches in the Seventeenth Century*[3] and the *Social and Economic Conditions in Wales and the Marches in the early Seventeenth Century*,[4] and with R. Flenley's *Calendar of the Register of the Queen's Majesty's Council in the Dominion and Principality of Wales and the Marches of the same, 1569–1591*,[5] will supply all the available information as to the origin, records, and functions of this body.

Within the limits of this pamphlet it has not been possible to do more than to touch upon the most obvious aspects of the Privy Council's work, and there are many others that will soon suggest themselves to any student of its history in the sixteenth and seventeenth centuries. The problems to investigate are almost innumerable, the way of the investigator is dark and difficult to find, for his information must be sought in many diverse places; to him indexes are often the most fallacious of signposts, and the mountain that he is seeking sometimes seems but a molehill when he has found it. Yet the solution of these problems must be undertaken if a just view is to be obtained of the two centuries which, above all others, mark a turning-point in the development of English society, English government, and English ideals.

[1] *The Council of the West. Trans. of the R. Hist. Soc.*, 4th Ser., vol. iv., pp. 62-80 (1921).

[2] 1904. This has a valuable bibliography.

[3] *E.H.R.*, vol. xxx., pp. 19-27 (January, 1915). This is largely based on a Register of the Council of Wales from 1586 to 1634 that was once among the Dovaston MSS., and is now in the B.M. (Egerton MS. 2882).

[4] *Trans. of the Hon. Soc. of Cymmrodorion*, Session 1916–1917 (1918).

[5] Cymmrodorion Record Series, No. 8 (1916). The original of this register is in the Bodleian (MS. Bodl. 904).

APPENDIX I

A list of some useful bibliographies of sixteenth and seventeenth century history. (Many of the modern works mentioned in later appendices have bibliographies relating to the special topics with which they deal.)

BRUCE, J.: Manuscript Catalogue of MSS. in the British Museum relating to the Privy Council and the Star Chamber (B.M. Add. MS. 28201). This is still of some value, though out of date. It may be supplemented by the subject catalogue in the manuscript room at the British Museum.

Cambridge History of English Literature (1908–1916). The bibliographies at the end of each volume are valuable, especially those to chap. 15 in vol. iv., chap. 14 in vol. v., and chaps. 8 and 9 in vol. vii.

Cambridge Modern History (1902–1912). The bibliographies to vol. i., chaps. 14, 15; vol. ii., chaps. 13-16; vol. iii., chaps. 8-10, 17, 18; vol. iv., chaps. 8-12, 15-19, 25; vol. v., chaps. 5, 8-11, 22, cover this period.

DAVIES, G.: *A Student's Guide to the Manuscripts relating to English History in the Seventeenth Century in the Bodleian Library* (1922).

FIRTH, C. H.: *Survey of Publications concerning English History in the Seventeenth Century. Revue Historique*, vol. lxi., 2, pp. 353-378; and vol. lxii., 1, pp. 95-116 (July and September, 1896).

FIRTH, C. H.: *The Development of the Study of Seventeenth Century History. Trans. of the R. Hist. Soc.*, 3rd Ser., vol. vii., pp. 25-48 (1913).

FIRTH, C. H.: *Survey of Seventeenth Century Sources. Trans. of the R. Hist. Soc.*, 3rd Ser., vol. viii., pp. 1-16 (1914).

FIRTH, C. H.: *Some Seventeenth Century Diaries and Memoirs. Scottish Historical Review*, vol. x., pp. 329-346 (July, 1913).

GARDINER, S. R., and MULLINGER, J. B.: *An Introduction to the Study of English History* (1903).

GEROULD, J. T.: *Sources of English History of the Seventeenth Century, 1603–1689, with a Selection of Secondary Material.* Research Publications of the Univ. of Minnesota, Bibliographical Series, No. 1 (1921). This is not really a bibliography, but a catalogue of one section of the Univ. of Minnesota's Library. So excellent, however, is the collection of works on the seventeenth century in this library that its catalogue is extremely valuable.

LOMAS, S. C.: *The State Papers of the Early Stuarts and the Interregnum. Trans. of the R. Hist. Soc.*, New Ser., vol. xvi., pp. 97-132 (1902).

LONGMAN'S *Political History of England* (1907–1910). Vols. v.-viii. contain fairly full bibliographies for this period.

ROUTLEDGE, F. J.: *Manuscripts at Oxford relating to the Later Tudors, 1547–1603. Trans. of the R. Hist. Soc.*, 3rd Ser., vol. viii., pp. 119-159 (1914).

APPENDIX II

A list of such of the contemporary collections of papers made by members of the Privy Council and the Councils of State, or by officials connected with them, as are likely to be of value for the history of the Privy Council in the sixteenth and seventeenth centuries. These are arranged alphabetically under the name or title by which each man is best known.

ARLINGTON, HENRY BENNET, EARL OF: He seems to have left no collection of papers behind him in private hands. The letters from Ralph Montague to Arlington (1668–1672) at Montague House (*Hist. MSS. Com., Buccleuch MSS.*, vol. i.) and the *Letters of State from Sir Henry Bennet* to Ormonde and Buckingham (1662–1667), printed by T. Brown in the *Miscellanea Aulica* (1702), contain interesting references to the Council and its intrigues, but the

Letters of the Earl of Arlington (2 vols., 1701) are almost wholly concerned with foreign affairs.

BAILLIE, ROBERT: His *Letters and Journals*, ed. by D. Laing in 3 vols. (1841), contain much information as to the Committee of Both Kingdoms.

BEALE, ROBERT. See p. 25.

BLATHWAYT, WILLIAM: His papers are B.M. Add. MSS. 9719-9768, 34348, 34351, 34352, 34354-34357, 37979-37992, 38694-38714, but the only two volumes of much direct value for the Privy Council are Add. MSS. 37991, 37992—the registers of his correspondence as secretary in attendance on William III. in the Netherlands, 1692–1701.

BUCKINGHAM, GEORGE VILLIERS, DUKE OF: Many of his papers passed into the hands of his secretary, John Packer, and thence into the possession of the Hon. G. M. Fortescue of Dropmore House, and were reported on by the Hist. MSS. Com. in the *2nd Rep., App.*, pp. 49-63; they are now in the Bodleian (MSS. Add. D. 109-122; see F. Madan: *A Summary Catalogue of Western MSS. in the Bodleian Library*, vol. v., pp. 544-545). Selections from these have been printed by S. R. Gardiner in the *Fortescue Papers*, Camden Soc., New Ser., No. 1 (1871). Other portions of Buckingham's correspondence are to be found in the Stirling-Howe-Drummond-Moray MSS. (*Hist. MSS. Com., 10th Rep., App. I.*); in B.M. Harl. MSS. 1580, 1581; in D. Dalrymple: *Memorials and Letters relating to the History of Britain in the reign of James I.* (2nd ed., 1766); and in *Cabala sive Scrinia Sacra* (1654 and 1663). These are chiefly valuable for foreign affairs, though they show the extent to which Buckingham managed foreign diplomacy without consulting the Council.

CÆSAR, SIR JULIUS. See p. 22.

CECIL, WILLIAM, LORD BURGHLEY. See pp. 17-18.

CECIL, ROBERT, EARL OF SALISBURY. See pp. 17-18.

CLARENDON, EDWARD HYDE, EARL OF. See pp. 18-19.

COKE, SIR JOHN. See pp. 20, 21.

CONWAY, SIR EDWARD. See p. 20.

COVENTRY, HENRY: Some of his correspondence is B.M. Add. MSS. 25117-25125, and there are further valuable papers in the Marquis of Bath's MSS. at Longleat (*Hist. MSS. Com., 4th Rep., App.,* pp. 228-236; but this is little more than a mere catalogue).

CRANFIELD, LIONEL, EARL OF MIDDLESEX: His papers are among the Earl De la Warr's MSS. at Knole Park (*Hist. MSS. Com., 4th Rep., App.,* pp. 276-317).

CROMWELL, OLIVER: *Letters and Speeches,* ed. by S. C. Lomas (3 vols., 1904). These contain a little in regard to the Council of State.

DANBY, THOMAS OSBORNE, EARL OF. See pp. 23-24.

DARTMOUTH, GEORGE LEGGE, BARON: His correspondence, which is most valuable between 1679 and 1689, is calendared in the *MSS. of Earl of Dartmouth,* vol. i. (*Hist. MSS. Com., 11th Rep., App. V.*). Vols. ii. and iii. are little good.

EDMONDES, SIR THOMAS: His papers are B.M. Stowe MSS. 166-178. Some are printed by T. Birch in his *Historical View of the Negotiations between the courts of England, France, and Brussels from the year 1592 to 1617* (1749). Stowe MSS. 166 and 167 have been printed by G. G. Butler in the *Edmondes Papers* (Roxburghe Club, 1913), but they are almost entirely concerned with foreign affairs.

EDWARD VI.: His "Journal" and "Articles on the Privy Council" are in B.M. Cotton MS., Nero CX. They have been printed by J. G. Nichols in the *Literary Remains of King Edward VI.,* 2 vols. (Roxburghe Club, 1857).

EGERTON, THOMAS, LORD ELLESMERE AND VISCOUNT BRACKLEY: His papers are divided between Bridgewater House, London, and the Bridgewater Trust Office at Walkden in Lancashire; the latter were reported on briefly by the Hist. MSS. Com. (*11th Rep., App. VII.,* pp. 126-167), but some of them have since been transferred to St. Gabriel's, California, U.S.A.   A selection of letters from the former collection was edited by J. P. Collier for the Camden Soc. (No. 12, 1840).   Both parts of this collection are useful for the Privy Council, and the papers at Walkden are in addition of value for the Council of Wales (of which the Earl of Bridgewater was President) and the Star Chamber (especially *Hist. MSS. Com., 11th Rep., App. VII.*, pp. 160-165).

ESSEX, ARTHUR CAPEL, EARL OF: The Essex papers (B.M. Stowe MSS. 200-217) are valuable for the relations of the Privy Council with the Irish Government and the Committee for Irish Affairs, and also for incidental notes on the members of the Privy Council by Essex's English correspondents during the years 1672–1677.   Selections have been edited for the Camden Soc. (vol. i., New Ser., No. 47, 1890; vol. ii., 3rd Ser., No. 24, 1913) by O. Airy and C. E. Pike.

FINCH, DANIEL, EARL OF NOTTINGHAM: Some of his papers were reported on by the Hist. MSS. Com. (Hatton MSS., *1st Rep., App.*, pp. 15-30); they are now in the British Museum among the Hatton-Finch MSS. (Add. MSS. 29548-29596), and are of very considerable value.   Letters from the Hatton-Finch MSS., addressed to Christopher, Viscount Hatton, were published by E. M. Thompson in the *Correspondence of the Family of Hatton* (Camden Soc., New Ser., Nos. 22 and 23, 1878); these contain incidental references of some value to the Privy Council.   There is also a great deal of Nottingham's correspondence among the Finch MSS.; this has been reported on to the end of the year 1690 by the Hist. MSS. Com. (*Finch MSS.*, vol. ii.), and is of very considerable value.

GUILFORD, FRANCIS NORTH, LORD: Some of his original papers and copies of others are to be found among Roger North's collections in the British Museum (Add. MSS. 32500-32527).   Add. MSS. 32518-32520 are decidedly valuable.

HALIFAX, GEORGE SAVILE, MARQUIS OF: The most extensive collection of his papers is to be found among the Spencer MSS. (*Hist. MSS. Com., 2nd Rep., App.*, pp. 12-20; a mere catalogue). Some idea of their great value can be gained from Miss Foxcroft's use of them in her *Life of Halifax*.

HARLEY, ROBERT, EARL OF OXFORD: Part of Harley's papers are in the possession of the Duke of Portland at Welbeck (*Hist. MSS. Com., Portland MSS.*, vols. iv. and v.; there are also some valuable news-letters among the earlier Harley papers in vol. iii., and vol. ii. has some interesting references to Cabinet and Council under Anne). The rest of his papers belong to the Marquis of Bath (*Hist. MSS. Com., Longleat MSS.*, vol. i.). Both these collections are exceedingly valuable for the inner history of the Cabinet at the beginning of the eighteenth century.

HAY, JAMES, BARON DONCASTER, EARL OF CARLISLE: His correspondence (1619–1636; B.M. Egerton MSS. 2592-2597) is disappointing, but some of the letters from London to Carlisle abroad are useful.

HYDE, HENRY, EARL OF CLARENDON; AND LAWRENCE, EARL OF ROCHESTER: Their correspondence, ed. by S. W. Singer (2 vols., 1828), contains a little of importance for the Privy Council, but is, on the whole, disappointing.

JAMES I.: *The Political Works of James I.*, ed. by C. H. McIlwain (1918), contains a few interesting references to James' view of the proper position of the Privy Council.

JENKINS, SIR LEOLINE: *The Life of Sir Leoline Jenkins . . . and a compleat series of letters from the beginning to the end of those two important treaties* (Cologne and Nymegen), by W. Wynne (2 vols., 1724), is very disappointing. There is also a large collection of Jenkins' papers in All Souls' College, Oxford, but it has little or nothing concerning the Privy Council.

LAUD, WILLIAM, ARCHBISHOP OF CANTERBURY: *The History of the Troubles and Tryal of the Most Reverend Father in God and Blessed Martyr, William Laud*, ed. by H. Wharton (1695), contains Laud's

Diary (pp. 1-67), which is of some value for the Privy Council and its committees.

MANCHESTER, HENRY MONTAGUE, VISCOUNT MANDEVILLE AND EARL OF: There are some valuable letters from him at the end of the reign of James I. and the beginning of that of Charles I. in the Montague Papers (*Hist. MSS. Com., Buccleuch MSS. at Montague House*, vol. i.).

MARY II.: *The Memoirs of Mary, Queen of England, 1689–1693*, ed. by R. Doebner (1886), contain much information as to the Cabinet.

NICHOLAS, EDWARD AND JOHN. See pp. 20, 21.

ORMONDE, JAMES, DUKE OF. See pp. 24-25.

PRESTON, RICHARD GRAHAM, VISCOUNT: His correspondence while he was ambassador to France (1682–1685) is among the MSS. of Sir F. Graham (*Hist. MSS. Com., 7th Rep., App., Pt. I.*). The letters from London to Preston in Paris contain a certain amount of useful information.

SADLER, SIR RALPH: His correspondence between 1559 and 1585 is in B.M. Add. MSS. 33591-33594, and transcripts of his correspondence in 1539 and 1543 are in B.M. Egerton MS. 2430 and Add. MSS. 31991, 33252, and 33252B. Many of these papers were printed in full, though not very accurately, in the *State Papers and Letters of Sir Ralph Sadler*, 2 vols., ed. by A. Clifford and W. Scott in 1809 (this supersedes the *Letters and Negotiations of Sir Ralph Sadler* that appeared in 1720); as far as 1547 these are calendared in the *Letters and Papers of Henry VIII.*, and the letters concerning his embassy of 1543 appear also in the *Hamilton Papers*. Sadler's papers are valuable mainly for the Privy Council's activities in connection with his embassies to Scotland.

SHAFTESBURY, ANTHONY ASHLEY COOPER, EARL OF. See p. 23.

SHREWSBURY, GEORGE TALBOT, EARL OF: A selection from his papers in the College of Arms was published by E. Lodge in his *Illustrations of British History* (3 vols., 1791). Some of the letters to

Shrewsbury contain valuable information as to Elizabeth's councillors.

Shrewsbury, Charles Talbot, Duke of. See pp. 21-22.

Southwell, Robert and Edward. See p. 25.

Thurloe, John. See pp. 19-20.

Vernon, James. See p. 22.

Walsingham, Sir Francis. See p. 20.

William III.: There is a considerable collection of letters from William III. to Bentinck, Earl of Portland (1677–1700), in the possession of the Duke of Portland at Welbeck; these have not yet been reported on by the Hist. MSS. Com., but transcripts of many of them were made for Sir James Mackintosh, and are now B.M. Add. MS. 34514; many of these were printed by P. Gromblot in the *Letters of William III. and Louis XIV. and of their Ministers*, 1697–1700 (1848). Mackintosh's collection of transcripts also includes copies of William III.'s letters to Heinsius, 1689–1702 (B.M. Add. MSS. 34504, 34505); some of these were printed by Ranke in the appendix to his *History of England principally in the Seventeenth Century* (English transl., 7 vols., 1875). Among the MSS. of Mr. F. J. Savile Foljambe there is a very valuable series of letters from James, Duke of York, to William (1678–1679, *Hist. MSS. Com., 15th Rep., App. V.*); this supplements William's correspondence printed in Groen van Prinsterer's *Archives ou Correspondance inédite de la Maison d'Orange Nassau*, and the numerous letters from James to William among the State Papers, Domestic.

Williamson, Sir Joseph. See p. 20.

Windebank, Sir Francis. See p. 20.

Winwood, Sir Ralph. See p. 21.

Worcester, Henry Somerset, Marquis of: His correspondence is among the Beaufort MSS. (*Hist. MSS. Com., 12th Rep., App. IX.*); there are some interesting notices of Privy Council meetings during the years 1678–1682.

APPENDIX III

A list of the contemporary collections of papers which were made by persons who were not members of the Privy Council, and which have some value for its history during the sixteenth and seventeenth centuries.

ASTON, SIR WALTER: His correspondence (B.M. Add. MSS. 36444-36451) includes many valuable letters from England to Aston while he was ambassador in Spain (1619–1638).

BACON, ANTHONY: His manuscripts are in Lambeth Library. T. Birch made transcripts from many of them (now B.M. Add. MSS. 4109-4124). These were published in his *Memoirs of the Reign of Queen Elizabeth* (2 vols., 1754).

BAGOT, RICHARD: His correspondence during the last quarter of the sixteenth century contains many letters of court news; it is now in the possession of Lord Bagot (*Hist. MSS. Com., 4th Rep., App.,* pp. 325-344).

BRADSHAW, RICHARD: Letters to him while he was agent at Hamburg and Copenhagen (1650–1658) are among the Farington MSS. (*Hist. MSS. Com., 6th Rep., App.,* pp. 426-444), and are valuable for the Council of State.

BULSTRODE, SIR RICHARD: Mr. T. E. P. Lefroy possessed a collection of letters written to him while he was agent at Brussels by many of the most important statesmen during the reigns of Charles II. and James II. It is reported on by the Hist. MSS. Com. (*1st Rep., App.,* p. 56), but so briefly that it is impossible to guess the value of these letters. The *Original Letters written to the Earl of Arlington by Sir Richard Bulstrode, Envoy at the Court of Brussels from King Charles II.,* ed. by E. Bysshe (1712), are of no value for this purpose.

CLARKE, SIR WILLIAM: His papers are in the library of Worcester College, Oxford, and selections from them, of considerable value for the Council of State, have been edited by C. H. Firth for the Camden Soc. (4 vols., New Ser., Nos. 49, 54; 3rd Ser., Nos. 61, 62, 1891–1901).

CORK, RICHARD BOYLE, EARL OF: His diary (1611–1643) and private letters (*c.* 1621–1646) have been edited by A. B. Grosart under the title of *The Lismore Papers* (1st Ser., 5 vols., 2nd Ser., 5 vols., 1886–1888). They are often valuable as showing the relations between a great noble and the Privy Council.

CROMWELL, HENRY: Many letters to him are in B.M. Lansd. MSS. 821-823. They contain much incidental reference to the Council of State.

DENBIGH, THE EARLS OF: There is a useful series of letters to Lord Feilding (later Earl of Denbigh), while he was ambassador in Italy (1635–1639), among Lord Denbigh's MSS. (*Hist. MSS. Com., 4th Rep., App.,* pp. 256-257). The same collection contains a valuable set of newsletters (May, 1691 to January, 1694) in French from a certain John Blancard (*Hist. MSS. Com., 7th Rep., Part I., App.,* pp. 196-221; *8th Rep., Part I., App.,* pp. 561-566; *MSS. of the Earl of Denbigh, Part V.;* introduction, pp. xv.-xviii.).

ELLIS, JOHN: As secretary to the Commissioners of Public Revenue in Dublin, and later under-secretary of state (1695–1705), he accumulated a large collection of papers and letters descriptive of court politics; these are now B.M. Add. MSS. 4194, 28875-28956. His correspondence between January, 1686 and December, 1688 has been published by the Hon. G. A. Ellis (*The Ellis Correspondence,* 2 vols., 1829).

FANSHAWE, SIR RICHARD: Letters addressed to him while he was ambassador to Portugal and Spain are to be found calendared among the *Heathcote MSS.* (*Hist. MSS. Com.,* 1899).

FLEMING, SIR DANIEL: His papers contain a very fine set of newsletters (possibly at first from Williamson's office) from 1667 to 1680 and 1688 to 1691 (*MSS. of S. H. Le Fleming of Rydal Hall; Hist. MSS. Com., 12th Rep., App. VII.*).

GAWDY: The Gawdy family papers are now B.M. Egerton MSS. 2713-2722, 2804, and B.M. Add. MSS. 27395-27399, 36989, 36990; the volumes now in the Egerton Collection have been reported on by the Hist. MSS. Com. (*7th Rep., App.*, pp. 518-530; 10*th Rep., App. II.*). I. H. Jeayes printed the *Letters of Philip Gawdy*, 1579–1616 (Roxburghe Club, 1906) very largely from Egerton MS. 2804.

HOLGATE, ROBERT, ARCHBISHOP OF YORK AND PRESI-DENT OF THE COUNCIL OF THE NORTH: Copies of many of his papers are to be found among the Tanner MSS. in the Bodleian Library (*e.g.*, MS. Tanner 90); they include many letters to and from the Council of Edward VI. Some of these papers have been printed in P. F. Tytler: *England under the Reigns of Edward VI. and Mary* (2 vols., 1839), and in the *E.H.R.* for July, 1894 (vol. ix., pp. 542-548).

PARRY, FRANCIS: *The Letters from the Secretaries of State and other persons in the reign of King Charles II. to Francis Parry, English Envoy to Portugal*, appeared in 1817. These letters run from October 23, 1668 to September 27, 1679, and contain occasional notes of action taken in the Council or its committees.

PEPYS, SAMUEL: His papers are in the Pepys Library of Magdalene College, Cambridge (calendered by J. R. Tanner; see p. 49) and in the Bodleian at Oxford (*e.g.*, MSS. Rawlinson, A. 170-195A, A. 464, C. 302, and C. 859; the Rawlinson MSS. also contain many other volumes which were in Pepys' possession, though they are not specifically called Pepys Papers). They contain a certain amount of information on the relation of the Privy Council with the Admiralty.

PRIOR, MATTHEW: His correspondence during the years 1685–1721 is at Longleat (*Hist. MSS. Com., Longleat MSS.*, vol. iii.). It throws some light on the Cabinet Council. This correspondence was used extensively by L. G. Wickham Legg in his *Life of Matthew Prior* (1921).

RADCLIFFE, SIR GEORGE: *The Life and Original Correspondence of Sir G. Radcliffe* was edited by T. D.

Whitaker in 1810. Radcliffe was Strafford's secretary, and his papers are decidedly valuable.

RUTLAND, EARLS OF: The Hist. MSS. Com. has reported on their papers at some length. Vol. i. of the *Rutland MSS.* is valuable owing to the many correspondents the Manners family had in London during the sixteenth and seventeenth centuries. Vol. iv. has an interesting series of letters between the Privy Council and the Earl of Rutland in 1549 about Scotch border business.

SANCROFT, WILLIAM, ARCHBISHOP OF CANTERBURY: His papers are in the Tanner MSS. in the Bodleian Library. J. Gutch printed many of them in his *Collectanea Curiosa* (2 vols., 1781); vol. i. contains an interesting account of the appearance of the seven Bishops before the Privy Council.

SCUDAMORE, JOHN, LORD: B.M. Add. MS. 11045 contains a useful series of newsletters written to Lord Scudamore during the years 1640–1641.

SIDNEY, ALGERNON: *The Letters of Algernon Sidney to Henry Savile, Ambassador in France* (1742), were written between February, 1679 and October, 1680, and have a considerable number of references to the Privy Council.

TREBY, SIR GEORGE: He was a distinguished Whig lawyer and chairman of the Committee of Secrecy, appointed to investigate the Popish Plot. His papers are among the Fitzherbert MSS. (*Hist. MSS. Com.*, 13*th Rep., App. VI.*).

APPENDIX IV

A list of miscellaneous general collections which contain matter of value for the history of the Privy Council in the sixteenth and seventeenth centuries, details of which have not been given in other appendices.

BIRCH, T.: From his transcripts were printed the *Court and Times of James I.* (2 vols., 1848), and the *Court and Times of Charles I.* (2 vols., 1848). They contain a large number of very valuable newsletters printed in full, but with many errors.

CAREW, GEORGE, EARL TOTNESS: J. Maclean edited the *Letters of George Lord Carew to Sir Thomas Roe, 1615–1617,* for the Camden Soc. (No. 76, 1860). They are in the nature of newsletters.

CARY, HENRY: *Memorials of the Civil War, 1646–1652* (2 vols., 1842). There is a little of value for the Council of State, but not much.

CHAMBERLAIN, JOHN: Some of his newsletters were edited by S. Williams for the Camden Soc. (*Letters written by John Chamberlain during the reign of Queen Elizabeth,* No. 79, 1861).

COTTON, SIR JOHN.   See p. 28.

DALRYMPLE, SIR JOHN: *Memoirs of Great Britain and Ireland* (2 vols. and Appendix, 1771–1788). The appendix contains a valuable collection of papers from 1660 to 1702.

ELLIS, SIR H.: *Original Letters* (1st Ser., 3 vols., 1825; 2nd Ser., 4 vols., 1827; 3rd Ser., 4 vols., 1846). This has some things of value—*e.g.,* letters from Robert Beale and Sir Thomas Elyot, and an Italian Relation.

GARDINER, S. R.: *The Constitutional Documents of the Puritan Revolution* (3rd ed., 1906). This has a few extracts of value for the Council of State.

GARDINER, S. R.: *Letters and other Documents illustrating the Relations between England and Germany, 1619–1620* (Camden Soc., No. 98, 1868), contains some valuable indications of the Privy Council's activity in foreign affairs.

HARDWICKE PAPERS: The original collection is now B.M. Add. MSS. 35349-36278. Selections from it were published in the *Hardwicke State Papers, 1501–1726* (2 vols., 1778). This is very miscellaneous, but contains a great deal of matter useful in regard to the Privy Council and the Cabinet (*cf.* especially the Somers Papers, 1689–1709).

HARGRAVE, FRANCIS: His manuscripts, now in the British Museum, are especially rich in sixteenth and seventeenth century manuscripts of legal interest, and contain a number of accounts of proceedings before the Privy Council or Star Chamber —*e.g.*, Hargrave MSS. 26, 27, 216, 226, 237, 249, 321, 404, 482, 489. There is a very brief printed catalogue.

HOUSEHOLD: *A Collection of Ordinances and Regulations for the Government of the Royal Household from Edward VI. to William and Mary.* Society of Antiquaries (1790). This contains some very important ordinances in connection with the Council, especially those of 1526.

MACKINTOSH, SIR JAMES: The collection of transcripts made by Sir J. Mackintosh for his *History of Great Britain from* 1688 *to* 1789 is now in the British Museum (Add. MSS. 34487-34526). In addition to copies of foreign ambassadors' despatches and of those of William III. (*q.v.*), it contains a volume of interesting newsletters from May, 1687 to December, 1688 (Add. MS. 34487).

MISCELLANEOUS MANUSCRIPT VOLUMES: In the British Museum: Harl. MS. 6987 contains a series of valuable letters on the Spanish adventure of Buckingham and Prince Charles in 1623, which have a good deal of interest for the Privy Council; Add. MS. 5756 (fol. 143) contains copies of warrants for the salaries of clerks of the Privy Council (1639–1685); Add. MS. 32323 is a precedent book of sixteenth-century Privy Council orders; Royal MS. 18, C. xxiv. is a docquet book of bills signed by King and Council as warrants for the Great Seal (1550–1553). In the Bodleian: MS. Ashmole 1729 (fols. 39-97) is a collection of James I.'s orders to the Privy Council immediately after Elizabeth's death.

NALSON, J. See p. 27.

NICHOLS, J. G.: *The Chronicle of Queen Jane.* Camden Soc., No. 48 (1850). This contains a calendar of State Papers of Lady Jane Grey (pp. 106-109) and of Mary (pp. 174-179), which are not in the *Calendar of S.P. Dom.*, 1547–1580.

NORTH, ROGER.   See p. 28.

PECK, FRANCIS: *Desiderata Curiosa* (2 vols. in one, 1779). This contains a considerable number of Privy Council letters, many of which are derived from the manuscripts of William Chaderton, Bishop of Chester.

PROCLAMATIONS: There are many collections: one in nine volumes at the Privy Council Office extending from Elizabeth to George II. (the volume, 1603–1613, has been lost); one among the manuscripts of the Earl of Portsmouth (*Hist. MSS. Com., 8th Rep., App., Pt. I.*, p. 61) giving the Privy Council proclamations and orders in regard to the business of the Mint from 1571 to 1584; the ordinances made by the Protector and Council of State in 1653–1654 are printed in C. H. Firth and R. S. Rait: *Acts and Ordinances of the Interregnum* (3 vols., 1911); the older printed collections have been superseded by R. R. Steele: *Bibliography of Royal Proclamations of the Tudor and Stuart Sovereigns and others published under authority, 1485–1714* (2 vols., 1910).   This gives, where possible, a summary of each proclamation, together with a reference to the original version if it exists.

PROTHERO, G. W.: *Select Statutes and other Constitutional Documents illustrative of the Reigns of Elizabeth and James I.* (4th ed., 1913) contains a few documents of value for the Privy Council and the Star Chamber.

RUSHWORTH, J.   See p. 27.

RYMER, THOMAS: *Foedera* (20 vols., 1727–1735).   This includes documents down to 1654, the last three volumes being compiled by Robert Sanderson; it does not, however, contain much of value for the Privy Council.

STATE PAPER OFFICE: There is a valuable series of papers bearing on the history of the State Paper Office calendared in the *30th Report of the Deputy Keeper of Public Records, App.,* pp. 212-293; it contains a good deal about the Privy Council and its relations with the State Paper Office.

SYDNEY LETTERS: Arthur Collins edited the *Letters and Memorials of State* commonly known as the *Sydney Letters* (2 vols., 1746); this is the correspondence of various members of the Sidney family from 1559 to 1663, and it contains a very considerable number of interesting letters to and from the Privy Council and the secretaries of state.

TANNER, J. R.: *Tudor Constitutional Documents, 1485–1603* (1922). This contains quite a useful selection of documents dealing with the Privy Council, the Star Chamber, the Court of Requests, and the Councils of Wales, the North, and the West (pp. 213-335).

WRIGHT, THOMAS: *Queen Elizabeth and her Times* (2 vols., 1838). This consists of a large number of letters, the originals of which are in the British Museum or the Cambridge University Library. Some of these are valuable for the history of the Privy Council.

APPENDIX V

A list of the more important collections of diplomatic correspondence from foreign ambassadors in England in print or in manuscript in this country, and valuable for the history of the Privy Council in the sixteenth and seventeenth centuries.

GENERAL.

CAMPANA DE CAVELLI, MARQUISE DE. See p. 32.
DAVENPORT, F. G. See p. 32.
FIRTH, C. H.: Series edited by. See p. 31.

BRANDENBURG.

BONET, FREDERICK: He was the resident in London for the Elector of Brandenburg from 1685 to 1696, and his original despatches were used by Ranke; some of them (1690–1695) are printed by him in the appendix to his *History of England principally in the Seventeenth Century* (English transl., 7 vols., 1875).

BONET, LOUIS FREDERICK: Transcripts of his despatches from 1696 to 1701, while he was resident in London, are B.M. Add. MS. 30000 (5 vols.).

SCHLEZER, J. F.: His despatches (1655–1659) while resident in London for the Elector of Brandenburg are printed in B. Erdmannsdörffer: *Urkunden und Actenstücke zur Geschichte des Kurfürsten Friedrich Wilhelm von Brandenburg*, vol. vii., pp. 705-826 (Berlin, 1877).

FRANCE.

BARILLON, PAUL: His despatches to Louis XIV. between December 7, 1684 and December 6, 1685 are printed in the appendix (pp. vii-cxlviii) to C. J. Fox's *History of the early Part of the Reign of James II.* (1808); other despatches are printed in the appendix to vol. i. of Sir J. Dalrymple's *Memoirs of Great Britain and Ireland* (1771–1788). His despatches, transcribed by Baschet for the P.R.O., are of great value.

BASCHET, ARMAND: Transcripts in the P.R.O. See p. 31.

BASSOMPIERRE, MARESCHAL DE: The *Négociations de Mareschal de Bassompierre envoyé Ambassadeur Extraordinaire en Angleterre de la part du Roy très-Chrestien, l'an* 1626, was published at Cologne in 1668. A manuscript version is among Colbert's transcripts (B.M. Add. MS. 30650). Part of it has been translated by J. W. Croker in the *Memoir of the Embassy of F. de Bassompierre* (1819).

BEAUMONT, CHRISTOPHE DE HARLAY, COMTE DE: Transcripts of his despatches during his embassy in England (1602–1605) are in B.M. King's MSS. 121-128 and B.M. Add. MSS. 30638–30641. P. Laffleur de Kermaingant in his *Mission de Christophe de*

Harlay, Comte de Beaumont (2 vols., Paris, 1895) gives valuable information as to Beaumont's relations with the Privy Council.

BELLAY, JEAN DE: V. L. Bourilly and P. de Vaissière in their *Ambassades en Angleterre de Jean de Bellay, September,* 1527 *to February,* 1529 (1905), give an account of his embassy and summarise many of his despatches, but they appear to contain little of value for the Privy Council.

BELLIÈVRE, POMPONNE DE AND PIERRE DE: Many of their letters (1646–1649) are printed in J. G. Fotheringham: *The Diplomatic Correspondence of Jean de Montereul and the Brothers de Bellièvre* (2 vols., Scottish History Soc., Nos. 29, 30, 1898, 1899); they are disappointing.

BLAINVILLE, JEAN DE VARIGNIES, SEIGNEUR DE: A copy of his " Négociation " containing his official correspondence during the years 1625 and 1626, when he was in England, is in B.M. King's MSS. 137, 138. B.M. Add. MS. 30651 is another copy.

BODERIE, ANTOINE LEFÈVRE DE LA: He was ambassador in England from April, 1606, to January, 1611, and copies of his despatches are to be found in B.M. King's MSS. 129, 130, and B.M. Add. MSS. 30642-30644; other copies are in the Bodleian (MSS. Carte, vols. 85 and 86, or vol. NNN).   Most of them were printed in the *Ambassades de M. le Fevre de la Boderie en Angleterre* (5 vols., 1750).   These are decidedly valuable for a rather obscure period.

BOISSISE, JEAN DE THUMERY, SIEUR DE: P. Laffleur de Kermaingant in his *Mission de Jean de Thumery, Sieur de Boissise,* 1598–1602 (2 vols., Paris, 1886), gives a history of the embassy in vol. i., while vol. ii. consists of relevant letters mostly from Henry IV. to Boissise; both vols. are of value for the Privy Council.

BORDEAUX-NEUFVILLE, ANTOINE DE: Copies of letters from him during the years 1657 and 1658 are in B.M. Add. MS. 31953 and B.M. Harl. MS. 4549, and some are also printed in the appendices to Guizot's *Histoire de la République d'Angleterre et de Cromwell* (2 vols., 1854), and his *Histoire du Protectorat de Richard Cromwell* (2 vols., 1856).

CASTILLON, LOUIS DE PERREAU, SIEUR DE: The *Correspondance Politique de MM. de Castillon et de Marillac, Ambassadeurs de France en Angleterre, 1537–1542*, ed. by J. Kaulek, L. Farges, and G. Lefèvre-Pontalis (Paris, 1885), contains many valuable references to the early Privy Council.

COMMINGES, JEAN BAPTISTE GASTON, COMTE DE: His "Relation d'Angleterre" is in B.M. Egerton MSS. 627, 1680, fol. 179; *cf.* also B.M. Egerton MS. 812. The extracts from his correspondence printed by J. J. Jusserand in *A French Ambassador at the Court of Charles II.* (1892) have very little value for the Privy Council.

CROULLE, M. DE: His letters from 1649 to 1651 are in B.M. Egerton MS. 1968.

EFFIAT, ANTOINE, MARQUIS DE: Copies of his despatches (1624–1625) are to be found in B.M. Harl. MSS. 4593-4597, B.M. King's MSS. 133-136, B.M. Add. MSS. 4150-4154, 30646-30649, and in the Bodleian (MS. Carte, vol. 82 or KKK).

ESTRADES, GODEFROI, COMTE DE: Some of his despatches during his embassy in England (July, 1661 to October, 1662) are printed in vol. i. of the *Lettres, Mémoires et Négociations de M. le Comte d'Estrades* (9 vols., 1743). Transcripts of his despatches for the same period, some of which are not printed, are in B.M. Egerton MS. 2071.

FONTENAY MAREUIL, M. DE: He was ambassador from 1630 to 1633, and he has left an interesting "Mémoire donné à M. de Chavigny, Secrétaire d'Etat le 25 Mars, 1634, sur l'état present de la cour d'Angleterre," printed in Michaud et Poujoulat: *Collection des Mémoires*, 2nd Ser., v., pp. 287-289. See also Ranke: *History of England principally in the Seventeenth Century*, vol. v., pp. 446-450 (English transl., 7 vols., 1875).

MAISSE, HURAULT DE: M. Prevost-Paradol describes
de Maisse's mission in his *Elisabeth et Henry IV.,
1595–1598* (1885).

MARILLAC, CHARLES DE.   See Castillon.

MIGNET, F. A. M.: In his *Négociations relatives à la
Succession d'Espagne sous Louis XIV.* (1835–1842)
he prints, among others, many despatches from the
French ambassadors in London during the reign
of Charles II.

MONTEREUL, JEAN DE.   See Bellièvre.

MOTHE FÉNÉLON, BERTRAND DE SALIGNAC, COMTE DE
LA: His correspondence was edited by C. P. Cooper
(*Correspondance Diplomatique de La Mothe-Fénélon*,
7 vols., 1838–1840); he was ambassador from 1568
to 1575.

NOAILLES, ANTOINE AND FRANCOIS DE: Despatches
from Antoine de Noailles are in the Bodleian (MSS.
Carte, vols. 87, 88, or OOO), and many letters from
him were published by R. Aubert de Vertot d'Aubeuf
in his *Ambassades de MM. de Noailles en Angleterre,
1552–1556* (5 vols., 1763).

SABRAN, MELCHIOR, COMTE DE: The " Livre des Négociations de M. Sabran, envoye resident en Angleterre
pour le service du Roy très-Chréstien depuis le
17 jour de Mai, 1644, au 8 Septembre, 1648," is
in the Bodleian (MS. Carte, vol. 84 or MMM).
Probably not of very great value for the Privy
Council.

SELVE, ODET DE: The *Correspondance politique d'Odet
de Selve*, 1546–1549, ed. by G. Lefèvre-Pontalis
(1888), is very valuable for his relations with the
Privy Council.

TALLARD, CAMILLE D'HOSTUN, COMTE DE: Some of his
letters from London to Louis XIV. are printed
in P. Gromblot's *Letters of William III. and Louis
XIV. and of their Ministers* (1848). Transcripts
of them are in the Mackintosh Collection (B.M.
Add. MS. 34492).   A. Legrelle quotes Tallard's
despatches extensively in his *La Diplomatie fran-
çaise et la succession d'Espagne* (6 vols., 1895–1899).

Tillières, Comte Leveneur de: The *Mémoires Inèdits du Comte Leveneur de Tillières*, ed. by C. Hippeau (1862), contain a very full account of England, *c.* 1618–1628.

Italian States.

Genoa—Bernardi, Francesco: His correspondence from September, 1651, to September, 1658, has been edited by C. Prayer, *Oliviero Cromwell della battaglia di Worcester alla sua morte* (*Atti della Società Ligure di Storia patria*, vol. xvi., Genoa, 1882).

Ottone, Carlo: His correspondence (1670-1674) has been printed by F. Poggi in the *Atti della Società Ligure di Storia patria* (vols. xlv., l., Genoa, 1914, 1923); it is not of great value for Privy Council history.

Milan: *Calendar of Milanese State Papers.* See pp. 30-31.

Papacy: *Calendar of Roman Papers* and Roman Transcripts at the P.R.O. See p. 30.

Transcripts from the Papal Registers relating to England, Scotland, and Ireland between 1216 and 1759 are to be found in B.M. Add. MSS. 15351-15400.

Adda, Count Ferdinand de: He was Papal nuncio to James II.; transcripts of his correspondence are in B.M. Add. MSS. 15395-15397. Extracts from his letters in the Papal Archives in Paris were made for Sir J. Mackintosh, and are now B.M. Add. MS. 34503.

Piedmont: Transcripts of the despatches of the Piedmontese envoys in England (1611–1614) are in B.M. Add. MS. 32023a-b.

Tuscany—Salvetti, Amerigo and Giovanni: Transcripts of their despatches in the Florentine archives from 1616 to 1679 are in B.M. Add. MS. 27962 (21 vols.). There is a very full report by the Hist. MSS. Com. (*11th Rep., App. I.*) on a translation of these despatches from April 11, 1625, to December 16, 1628, in the possession of H. D. Skrine. These despatches are very valuable for the history of the Privy Council and the Council of State.

Venice—Barozzi, N., and Berchet, G. See p. 30.
Calendars of Venetian State Papers, Report on Venetian Archives, and Venetian Transcripts in P.R.O. See p. 30.

Giustiniano, Sebastiano: A translation of some of his despatches was published by R. Brown under the title of *Four Years at the Court of Henry VIII.* (2 vols., 1854). They run from 1515 to 1519.

Michiel, Giovanni: His despatches were printed in full in P. Friedmann: *Les Dépêches de Giovanni Michiel, ambassadeur de Venise en Angleterre, 1554–1557* (1869).

The Netherlands.

Transcripts of State Papers and Correspondence in regard to England from the Hague Archives from 1576 to 1764 are in B.M. Add. MS. 17677 (102 vols.).

Transcripts of despatches from the Dutch ambassador in London between 1685 and 1688 are among Sir J. Mackintosh's papers (B.M. Add. MSS. 34507-34512).

Spain and the Empire.

Calendars of Spanish State Papers and Transcripts at the P.R.O. and B.M. See p. 29.

Cardeñas, Alonzo de: Some of his despatches are printed in the appendices to Guizot's *Histoire de la République d'Angleterre et de Cromwell* (2 vols., 1854) and his *Histoire de Protectorat de Richard Cromwell* (2 vols., 1856).

Gondomar, Don Diego Sarmiento de Acuña, Conde de: *Cinco Cartas*, ed. by Don Pascual de Gayangos (Madrid, 1869). The second letter is useful.

Kervyn de Lettenhove. See pp. 29-30.

Navarrete, M. F. de. See p. 29.

Renard, Simon: Vol. iv. of the *Papiers d'Etat du Cardinal de Granvelle*, ed. by C. Weiss (9 vols., 1841–1852), contains some very interesting despatches from Renard.

APPENDIX VI

A list of the main diaries, autobiographies, memoirs, contemporary histories, and biographies that are valuable for the history of the Privy Council in the sixteenth and seventeenth centuries.

AILESBURY, THOMAS BRUCE, SECOND EARL OF: *Memoirs*, ed. by W. E. Buckley (Roxburghe Club, 1890). This has much about the ministers of Charles II. and James II., but it was not written till 1728, and then practically entirely from memory.

ANGLESEY, ARTHUR ANNESLEY, EARL OF: Part of his diary is in the possession of Lieut.-Gen. Lyttelton Annesley, and has been reported on by the Hist. MSS. Com. (13*th Rep., App. VI.*, pp. 261-278); his attendances at the Council Board between 1671 and 1675 are referred to.   A second volume carrying the diary down to 1684 is B.M. Add. MS. 18730.

BURNET, GILBERT.   See pp. 32-33.

CARY, ROBERT, EARL OF MONMOUTH: *Memoirs* (1759), also ed. by G. H. Powell for the King's Classics (1902).   There are several very interesting references to the Privy Council's action.

CLARENDON, EDWARD HYDE, EARL OF.   See p. 32.

COWPER, WILLIAM, FIRST EARL: *Private Diary*, ed. by E. C. Hawtrey (Roxburghe Club, 1833).   Very valuable for Cabinet meetings from October, 1705, to September, 1710.

GOODMAN, GODFREY: *The Court of King James I.*, ed. by J. S. Brewer (2 vols., 1839).   Vol. i. contains some interesting references to James' ministers; vol. ii. consists of illustrative letters added by Brewer from originals in the Cotton, Harleian, and Tanner collections.

JAMES II.: *The Life of James II.*, ed. by J. S. Clarke (2 vols., 1816), has some value for the court intrigues that surrounded James under Charles II. and during his own reign.   See Ranke: *A History of England, principally in the Seventeenth Century* (English transl., 7 vols., 1875), vol. vi., pp. 29-45, for a discussion of the real nature of this so-called autobiography. The original manuscript version is among the Stuart MSS. at Windsor, and extracts from the materials from which it was compiled are given in J. Macpherson's *Original Papers* (2 vols., 1775).

LAUD, WILLIAM, ARCHBISHOP OF CANTERBURY: P. Heylyn's *Cyprianus Anglicus* (1668) is a life of Laud by his chaplain, but the references in it to the Privy Council and the Foreign Committee are disappointing. See also under Laud, on p. 61.

LUDLOW, EDMUND: His *Memoirs* have been edited by C. H. Firth (2 vols., 1894), and have considerable value for the Councils of State.

LUTTRELL, NARCISSUS. See p. 33.

MORICE, RALPH: He was Cranmer's secretary, and wrote an interesting account of the Council's attack on Cranmer in 1545. It is printed in the *Narratives of the Days of the Reformation*, ed. by J. G. Nichols (Camden Soc., No. 77, 1859, pp. 254-259).

NAUNTON, SIR ROBERT: His *Fragmenta Regalia* (1641) contains character sketches of the chief men of Elizabeth's reign. It was reprinted in the *Harleian Miscellany* (ed. by T. Park, 10 vols., 1808–1813), vol. ii., pp. 81-108, and in Arber's English Reprints, No. 20 (1870).

NORTH, ROGER: *Lives of the Norths.* See p. 34.

NORTH, ROGER: *Examen* (1740). This is a criticism of White Kennett's *History of England;* it has some interesting matter regarding the Privy Council under Charles II.

PEPYS, SAMUEL: His *Diary* (ed. by H. B. Wheatley, 10 vols., 1893–1899) contains references to the meetings of the Privy Council and its committees (some of these are very interesting—*e.g.,* that on February 27, 1664, 1665), and a great deal as to the intrigues at court.

RERESBY, SIR JOHN. See p. 33.

SHERIDAN, THOMAS: His *Historical Account of some Remarkable Matters* (written in 1702) is printed by the Hist. MSS. Com. in the *Stuart Papers*, vol. vi., pp. 1-75; it is of some value for the Privy Council under James II.

SIDNEY, HENRY, EARL OF ROMNEY: His *Diary* was edited by R. W. Blencowe (2 vols., 1843). It contains many letters inserted to illustrate the diary, and is decidedly valuable for the Privy Council and its committees from 1679 to 1685.

TEMPLE, SIR WILLIAM.   See pp. 33-34.

UNDERHILL, EDWARD: His *Autobiography* was included by J. G. Nichols in the *Narratives of the Days of the Reformation* (Camden Soc., No. 77, 1859); it contains an interesting account of his appearance before the Council (pp. 138-144).

VENABLES, GENERAL ROBERT: *The Narrative of General Venables*, ed. by C. H. Firth for the Camden Soc. (3rd Ser., No. 60, 1900), contains a certain amount as to the activities of the Council of State in connection with the Jamaican Expedition.

WARWICK, SIR PHILIP: His *Memoires of the reigne of King Charles I., with a continuation to the happy restauration of King Charles II.* (1701), is of some value for Charles I.'s chief ministers.

WHITELOCKE, BULSTRODE.   See p. 33.

WILBRAHAM, SIR ROGER: His *Journal*, ed. by H. S. Scott, is in the *Camden Misc.*, vol. x. (Camden Soc., 3rd Ser., No. 4, 1902). It notes several meetings of the Privy Council at the end of the reign of Elizabeth and the beginning of that of James I., and the discussions therein.

WILLIAMS, JOHN, ARCHBISHOP OF YORK.   See p. 34.

WILLIAMSON, SIR JOSEPH: His *Journal* (1667–1673) is in the State Papers, Domestic (S.P. Dom., Charles II., ccxxxi., ccliii., cclxxi.; S.P. Dom., cccxixa, and S.P. Misc., ccxv., are very fragmentary).

APPENDIX VII

A list of contemporary accounts of the Privy Council, Star Chamber, and Court of Requests.

A *Vindication of the Rights of the Commons of England,* printed in the *Somers Tracts,* vol. xi., pp. 276-315, contains a section on the " Establishment and Use of the King's Councils " (pp. 292-294).

BACON, FRANCIS: His essay *Of Counsel* (ed. by S. H. Reynolds from the edition of 1625) is very valuable.

CÆSAR, SIR JULIUS: *The Ancient State, Authoritie, and Proceedings of the Court of Requests* (1597). There is a copy of this work in B.M. Lansd. MS. 125 with Cæsar's own annotations.

COKE, SIR EDWARD: *The Fourth Part of the Institutes of the Laws of England* (1644) contains descriptions of the Privy Council, the Star Chamber, and the Court of Requests.

COTTON, ISAAC: The original of his treatise on the Star Chamber (1622) is B.M. Stowe MS. 418; B.M. Lansd. MS. 639 is another copy.

CROMPTON, RICHARD: *L'Authoritie et Jurisdiction des Courts de la Majestie de la Roygne* (1594). The chapter on the Star Chamber (pp. 29-41) is translated in *Star Chamber Cases, showing what causes properly belong to the cognizance of that Court* (1630, 1641, reprinted by F. F. Heard in 1881).

DEFOE, DANIEL: A paper by him printed in *E.H.R.,* vol. xxii., pp. 130-143 (1907), contains a fair amount in regard to the Cabinet; it dates from c. 1704.

FAUNT, NICHOLAS: *Discourse touching the Office of Principal Secretary of Estate.* This was written in 1592, and was printed by C. Hughes in *E.H.R.,* vol. xx., pp. 499-508 (July, 1905); this has something about the Secretary's duties in relation to the Privy Council.

HAWARD, JOHN: *Les Reportes del Cases in Camera Stellata,* ed. by W. P. Baildon (1894). This has a valuable introduction.

HUDSON, WILLIAM: His *Treatise of the Court of Star Chamber* (written *c.* 1620) has been very badly printed in the *Collectanea Juridica*, vol. ii., pp. 1-240 (ed. by F. Hargrave, 2 vols., 1791). The best manuscript version of this is B.M. Add. MS. 11681; this was made by his son in 1634. There are many other manuscript copies in the B.M.

LAMBARDE, WILLIAM: *Archeion* (completed about 1591, published in 1635) has valuable sections on the Council, the Star Chamber, and the Court of Requests. See also B.M. Add. MSS. 4521.

MILL, WILLIAM: His "Discourse concerning the Antiquity of the Star Chamber" is B.M. Hargrave MS. 216.

RALEIGH, SIR WALTER: The *Cabinet Council* in his *Works* (1829 edition), vol. viii., p. 37, is a general treatise on the State, with chapters on "councils and councillors in general" (pp. 44-45), "particular councils" (pp. 45-46), and "the prince's intimate councillors and ministers of state with their several requisites" (pp. 54-58).

SMITH, SIR THOMAS: *De Republica Anglorum*, ed. by L. Alston (1906, written *c.* 1583), contains sections on the Privy Council, the Star Chamber, and the Court of Requests.

SPANHEIM, BARON EZEKIEL VON: His *Account of the English Court in* 1704 was printed in *E.H.R.*, vol. ii., p. 757 (1887), and is useful for the Cabinet.

APPENDIX VIII

List of books and articles dealing with the Cabinet and the conditions within the Council during the sixteenth and seventeenth centuries.

ADAMS, G. B. See p. 39.

ANSON, W. R. See pp. 36, 39.

BLAUVELT, M. T. See p. 38.

CARLYLE, E. I. See p. 38.

CORBETT, J. S.: *Queen Anne's Defence Committee* in the *Monthly Review* for May, 1904 (pp. 55-65). This is an account of the Secret Committee that acted from May, 1702, to January, 1703, and probably till much later.

DAVIES, G.: *Council and Cabinet, 1679–1688. E.H.R.,* vol. xxxvii., pp. 47-66 (January, 1922). This supplements Turner's articles on the same subject.

GRANT, W. L., AND MUNRO, J.   See p. 38.

JENKS, E.: *The Constitutional Experiments of the Commonwealth* (1890).

LEARNED, H. B.: *The History of the Significance of the term Cabinet in England and the United States. American Political Science Review,* vol. iii., p. 329 (1909).

MICHAEL, W.: *Englische Geschichte in achtzehnten Jahrhundert,* vol. i. (1896), and see p. 39.

MORGAN, W. T.: *English Political Parties and Leaders in the Reign of Queen Anne, 1702–1710* (1920).

MORGAN, W. T.: *The Ministerial Revolution of 1710 in England.   Political Science Quarterly,* vol. xxxvi., pp. 184-210 (June, 1921).

NOTESTEIN, W.   See p. 38.

READ, CONYERS: *Factions in the English Privy Council under Elizabeth.   American Historical Assoc. Reports* (1911).   Rather slight, but interesting.

READ, CONYERS: *Walsingham and Burghley in Queen Elizabeth's Privy Council.   E.H.R.,* vol. xxviii., pp. 34-58 (January, 1913).

SALOMON, F.: *Geschichte des letzten Ministeriums Königin Annas von England* (1894).

TEMPERLEY, H. W. V.   See pp. 38, 39.

TORRENS, W. M.   See p. 38.

TURNER, E. R.: *The Origin of the Cabinet Council. E.H.R.,* vol. xxxviii., pp. 171-205 (April, 1923).

TURNER, E. R.: *Committees of the Council and the Cabinet, 1660–1688.   A.H.R.,* vol. xix., pp. 772-793 (July, 1914).

TURNER, E. R.: *The Privy Council of 1679.   E.H.R.,* vol. xxx., pp. 251-270 (April, 1915).

TURNER, E. R.: *The Development of the Cabinet, 1688–1760.* Part I., *A.H.R.*, vol. xviii., pp. 751-768 (July, 1913); Part II., *A.H.R.*, vol. xix., pp. 27-43 (October, 1913).

TURNER, E. R.: *Privy Council Committees, 1688–1760.* *E.H.R.*, vol. xxxi., pp. 545-572 (October, 1916).

TURNER, E. R.: *The Lords of the Committee of the Council.* *A.H.R.*, vol. xxii., pp. 90-94 (October, 1916).

TURNER, E. R.: *The Lords Justices of England.* *E.H.R.*, vol. xxix., pp. 453-476 (July, 1914).

TURNER, E. R.: *The Cabinet in the Eighteenth Century.* *E.H.R.*, vol. xxxii., pp. 192-203 (April, 1917). This deals only with the eighteenth century, but it should be read with the other articles.

WALLIS, J. P.: *Cromwell's Constitutional Experiments.* *Nineteenth Century*, vol. xlvii., p. 443 (March, 1900).

APPENDIX IX

A list of such non-contemporary biographies as are useful for the history of the Privy Council in the sixteenth and seventeenth centuries. (The *Dictionary of National Biography* should always be consulted, if only for the bibliographical information given at the end of each article.)

BARBOUR, V.: *Henry Bennet, Earl of Arlington* (1913). See pp. 40-41.

BEAVEN, M. L. R.: *Sir William Temple* (1908). This is disappointing; the account of Temple's share in the Council of 1679 is superficial.

BREWER, J. S.: *Henry VIII.* (2 vols., 1884); this is really a general history reprinted from the introductions to the first four volumes of the *Letters and Papers.* There is something in regard to Henry's ministers, but much the greatest attention is given to foreign policy.

CARTE, T.: *An History of the Life of James, Duke of Ormonde* (3 vols., 1735–1736). This is mostly concerned with Irish affairs, but there is something as to Ormonde's position at court during Charles II.'s reign; vol. iii. is a collection of illustrative documents.

CHRISTIE, W. D.: *A Life of Anthony Ashley Cooper, First Earl of Shaftesbury* (2 vols., 1871). Rather disappointing.

COURTENAY, T. P.: *Memoirs of the Life, Works, and Correspondence of Sir William Temple* (2 vols., 1836). This is quite good for the events of 1679.

DEVEREUX, W. B.: *Lives and Letters of the Devereux, Earls of Essex* (2 vols., 1853). The life of Robert, Earl of Essex, is of some value, because of its account of the contest for power with Robert Cecil.

FIRTH, C. H.: *Oliver Cromwell and the Rule of the Puritans in England* (1909). Rather disappointing so far as the Council of State is concerned.

FOXCROFT, H. C.: *Life and Letters of Sir George Savile, Bart., First Marquis of Halifax* (2 vols., 1898). See p. 40.

FRIEDMANN, P.: *Anne Boleyn* (2 vols., 1884). This has something to say of the parties within the Council.

GARDINER, S. R.: *Oliver Cromwell* (1901). This tells one rather less than might be expected about the Council of State.

HARRIS, F. R.: *Life of Edward Mountagu, First Earl of Sandwich* (2 vols., 1912). See p. 40.

HOSMER, J. K.: *The Life of Young Sir Henry Vane* (1888). This has a certain amount about the Council of State and its committees, but gives practically no references.

HUME, M. A. S.: *The Great Lord Burghley* (1898). This is rather poor on the subject of Burghley's connection with the Council; it gives most attention to foreign affairs.

KENNEDY, W. M.: *Life of Parker* (1908). This is interesting mainly for the ecclesiastical side of the Council's activities.

LISTER, T. H.: *Life and Administration of Edward, First Earl of Clarendon* (3 vols., 1837–1838). This is quite useful; the third volume consists of illustrative documents.

MASSON, D.: *The Life of John Milton* (7 vols., 1871–1894).   See p. 40.

MERRIMAN, R. B.: *The Life and Letters of Thomas Cromwell* (2 vols., 1902).

NICOLAS, N. H.: *Life of William Davison* (1823).   See p. 40.

POLLARD, A. F.: *Henry VIII.* (1905).   See p. 40.

POLLARD, A. F.: *England under Protector Somerset* (1900).   See p. 40.

POLLARD, A. F.: *Thomas Cranmer* (1904).   This contains a certain amount as to his relations with the Council.

SPEDDING, J.: *The Life and Letters of Francis Bacon* (7 vols., 1861–1872).   See p. 40.

STÄHLIN, K.: *Sir Francis Walsingham und seine Zeit* (1908).   Only the first volume has so far appeared; this goes down to 1573, and is useful for the activities of the Privy Council in connection with foreign affairs.

STEBBING, W.: *Sir Walter Raleigh* (new ed., 1899).   This has some value for the intrigues at court between Raleigh and Sir Robert Cecil.

STRYPE, J.: For his biographies, see p. 35.

TRAILL, H. D.: *Lord Strafford* (1889).   A brief but interesting biography.

APPENDIX X

A list of such monographs as are not mentioned in other appendices, and have some value for the history of the Privy Council in the sixteenth and seventeenth centuries.

Lady Arabella Stuart and the Venetian Archives.   Edinburgh Review, vol. clxxxiv. (October, 1896).   This gives an account of her appearance before the Privy Council.

BEKKER, E.: *Elisabeth und Leicester, 1560–1562.* Giessener Studien, Heft 5. This describes Leicester's position in the Privy Council.

BUSCH, W.: *Der Sturz des Cardinals Wolsey.* Historisches Taschenbuch, Sechste Folge, ix., pp. 39-114. This throws some light on the position of Henry's ministers between October, 1528, and December, 1530.

CATTERALL, R. C. H.: *The Failure of the Humble Petition and Advice.* A.H.R., vol. ix., pp. 36-65 (October, 1903). This says something of the position of the parties in the Council of State in 1657–1658.

DODDS, M. H. AND R.: *The Pilgrimage of Grace and the Exeter Conspiracy* (1915). This is useful, not only for the Council of the North, but also for details as to the Pilgrims' attempt to dictate the membership of Henry's Council.

EVANS, F. M. G.: *The Principal Secretary of State* (Manchester Historical Series, 1923). This is of very considerable value for the history of the Privy Council during the period 1558-1680; it has a good bibliography (Appendices I. and V.).

GORDON, M. D.: *The Collection of Ship-money in the Reign of Charles I. Trans. of the R. Hist. Soc.,* 3rd Ser., vol. iv., pp. 141-162.

KENT, C. B. R.: *The Early History of the Tories from 1660 to 1702* (1908). This has a little to say in regard to the Cabinet and the party system, but it is not very reliable.

NICHOLS, J.: *The Progresses and Public Processions of Queen Elizabeth* (3 vols., 1821–1823); *The Progresses, Processions, and Magnificent Festivities of King James the First* (4 vols., 1828).

APPENDIX XI

A list of modern works dealing with the relations of the Privy Council and the colonies.

For the works of C. M. Andrews, G. L. Beer, M. P. Clarke, O. M. Dickerson, C. S. S. Higham, H. L. Osgood, W. T. Root, E. B. Russell, A. M. Schlesinger, see pp. 42-44.

BIEBER, R. P.: *The Lords of Trade and Plantations, 1675–1696* (1919). I have had no opportunity of reading this book, and therefore cannot estimate its value.

COLLINS, E. D.: *Studies in the Colonial Policy of England, 1672–1680. American Historical Assoc. Reports* (1900). This deals with the activities of the Council of State and of the Privy Council in regard to the provision of labour in the West Indies.

GRANT, W. L., AND MUNRO, J.: Introductions to vols. i. and ii. of the *Acts of the Privy Council, Colonial,* and C. M. Andrews' review thereof. See pp. 12, 38.

HARRIS, F. R.: *Life of Edward Montagu, First Earl of Sandwich.* See p. 40.

HAZELTINE, H. D.: *Appeals from Colonial Courts to the King in Council, with especial reference to Rhode Island.* Papers from the Historical Seminary of Brown University, No. 7, pp. 299-350 (1896). Interesting, but wholly from printed sources.

KAYE, P. L.: *The Colonial Executive prior to the Restoration.* Johns Hopkins Univ. Studies in Historical and Political Science, No. 18 (1900).

KAYE, P. L.: *Colonial Administration under Lord Clarendon.* Johns Hopkins Univ. Studies in His torical and Political Science, No. 23 (1905).

KELLOGG, L. P.: *The American Colonial Charter. American Historical Assoc. Report for* 1903, vol. i. This is decidedly good on the Board of Trade.

MACQUEEN, J.: *A Practical Treatise on the Appellate Jurisdiction of the House of Lords and the Privy*

Council (1842). The section on the Privy Council (pp. 671-773), though largely concerned with modern procedure, has some useful historical data and a valuable appendix of documents (pp. 800-808).

APPENDIX XII

A list of some of the modern works on economic history during the sixteenth and seventeenth centuries, which are also valuable for the history of the Privy Council during that period.

BEER, G. L.: *The Commercial Policy of England towards the American Colonies.* Columbia College Studies in History, Economics, and Public Laws, vol. iii., No. 2 (1893). This is the first sketch of his later works, *The Origins of the British Colonial System* (1908) and *The Old Colonial System* (1912), for which see p. 44. Embodied in the first of these is much of his essay on *Cromwell's Policy in its Economic Aspects*, which appeared in the *Political Science Quarterly*, vol. xvi., pp. 582-611, and vol. xvii., pp. 46-70; this is of some value for the Council of State, though one cannot always agree with Beer's conclusions.

BIRDWOOD, SIR G., AND FOSTER, W.: *The Register of Letters, etc., of the Governour and Company of Merchants of London trading into the East Indies,* 1600–1619 (1893), prints in full a few letters from and petitions to the Privy Council.

CHURCHILL, E. F.: *The Dispensing Power and the Defence of the Realm. Law Quarterly Review,* vol. xxxvii., pp. 412-441 (October, 1921). This contains a good deal as to the Privy Council's activities in connection with the navigation policy.

CUNNINGHAM, W. See p. 44.

DIETZ, F. C.: *English Government Finance,* 1485–1558. Univ. of Illinois Studies in Social Sciences, vol. ix., No. 3 (1920). This says a little about the Council's control of finance under Edward VI.

Durham, F. H.: *The Relation of the Crown to Trade under James I. Trans. of the R. Hist. Soc.*, New Ser., vol. xiii., pp. 199-247 (1899).

Foster, W.: *Court Minutes of the East India Company*, 1635–1659, a continuation of the Eastern series of the calendars of State Papers, Colonial (see pp. 41-42). These contain a little as to the Privy Council's relations with the East India Company's trade.

Gonner, E. C. K.: *The Progress of Inclosure during the Seventeenth Century. E.H.R.*, vol. xxiii., pp. 477-501 (July, 1908).

Leonard, E. M.: *The Inclosure of Common Fields in the Seventeenth Century. Trans. of the R. Hist. Soc.*, New Ser., vol. xix., pp. 101-146 (1905).

Leonard, E. M.: *The Early History of English Poor Relief* (1900). See p. 44.

Price, W. H.: *The English Patents of Monopoly* (1906).

Scott, W. R.   See pp. 44-45.

Skeel, C. A. J.: *The Canary Company. E.H.R.*, vol. xxxi., pp. 529-544 (October, 1916). This shows the activity of the Privy Council in 1665-1667 in the supervision of trade.

Stevens, H.: *The Dawn of British Trade to the East Indies*, 1599–1603 (1886). This prints a good many petitions, etc., to the Privy Council.

Tawney, R. H.: *The Agrarian Problem in the Sixteenth Century* (1912).

Unwin, G.   See p. 44.

APPENDIX XIII

A list of MSS. and later works illustrating the Privy Council's local activities in the sixteenth and seventeenth centuries. (The Privy Council Register, the State Papers, Domestic, and other principal sources already mentioned are not repeated here.)

Beard, C. A.   See p. 46.

Borders: The MSS. of the Earl of Crawford and Balcarres at Dunecht (*Hist. MSS. Com., 2nd Rep., App.*, pp. 181-182) contain a volume of the proceedings of the royal commission of 1605; this shows the activity of the Privy Council in the settlement of the Scottish borders and the expulsion of the Grahams, and the relation of the commission to the central body.

BUND, J. W. WILLIS: *The Diary of H. Townshend*, 1640–1663 (2 vols., 1916–1920). This includes a considerable number of documents of local interest and a valuable introduction by the editor giving, *inter alia*, a very good account of the levying of ship-money and subsidies in Worcestershire.

CHESTER. See p. 45.

DEVONSHIRE: The MSS. of the Duke of Somerset (*Hist. MSS. Com.*, 15th Rep., App. VII., pp. 2-62) contain many Privy Council orders for the defence of Devonshire from 1586 to 1613.

ESSEX: The MSS. of G. A. Lowndes (*Hist. MSS. Com.*, 7th Rep., App., Pt. I.) contain a considerable number of Privy Council letters of the later sixteenth and early seventeenth centuries in regard to Essex matters.

EXETER. See p. 45.

FOLJAMBE: The MSS. of F. J. Savile Foljambe (*Hist. MSS. Com.*, 15th Rep., App. V., pp. 1-123) contain a " Book of the Musters," which shows the activity of the Privy Council in the defence of the realm during the years 1571–1577, 1583–1590, and 1599.

GLOUCESTER: The MSS. of the Corporation of Gloucester (*Hist. MSS. Com.*, 12th Rep., App. IX., pp. 473-518) contain a letter book for 1619–1660, showing much correspondence with the Privy Council and the Council of State.

GROSS, C.: *A Bibliography of British Municipal History* (1897). A valuable critical guide.

HAMILTON, A. H. A.: *Quarter Sessions from Queen Elizabeth to Queen Anne* (1878). He quotes a considerable number of Privy Council letters and orders mainly drawn from the Devon Quarter Sessions

Records, and discusses the Privy Council's activity in local affairs.

HUMPHREYS, A. L.: *A Handbook to County Bibliography* (1917). This is a very valuable guide to the multitudinous books and articles on English local history.

KENT: B.M. Add. MS. 34218 contains copies of a number of Privy Council letters in regard to local affairs in Kent, made for Sir Francis Fane.

LANCASHIRE: *Lancashire Quarter Sessions Records*, vol. i., 1590–1606 (Chetham Soc., 1917). This has a valuable introduction by Professor J. Tait.

LEICESTER: The Hall Papers of the borough of Leicester, 1574–1685 (*Hist. MSS. Com., 8th Rep., App., Pt. I.*, pp. 430–441), contain a fair number of Privy Council letters.

LONDON. See p. 45.

MIDDLESEX: The Middlesex County Records contain a book of Council orders concerning the plague (1661–1666).

PLYMOUTH. See p. 45.

RYE, CORPORATION OF. See p. 45.

RYE, W. See pp. 46-47.

SOUTHAMPTON: The MSS. of Southampton (*Hist. MSS. Com., 11th Rep., App. III.*) show very plainly the great activity of the Privy Council in municipal affairs. *The Assembly Books of Southampton*, 2 vols., 1602–1608 and 1609–1610 (1917–1920), have been edited by J. W. Horrocks for the Southampton Record Soc., and R. C. Anderson has edited a volume of *Letters of the Fifteenth and Sixteenth Centuries from the Archives of Southampton* (Southampton Record Soc., 1921).

SUFFOLK. See p. 46.

SUSSEX. See p. 46.

THOMSON, G. S.: *Lords-Lieutenants in the Sixteenth Century* (1923). This describes fairly fully how the Council used the Lords-Lieutenants as part of the domestic, and especially of the military, administration of the country.

THOMSON, G. S.: *The Origin and Growth of the Office of Deputy-Lieutenant. Trans. of the R. Hist. Soc.,* 4th Ser., vol. v., pp. 150-166 (1922). This says something of the Deputy-Lieutenant's relations with the Privy Council.

APPENDIX XIV

A list of modern works that are valuable for the relation of the Privy Council with ecclesiastical affairs in the sixteenth and seventeenth centuries.

BROWN, L. F.: *The Political Activities of the Baptists and Fifth Monarchy Men in England during the Interregnum* (1911). This is valuable for the attempts of the Council of State to repress these movements. It has also a good bibliography.

BURNET, G.: *The History of the Reformation of the Church of England* (7 vols., 1865). See p. 35.

DIXON, R. W. See p. 47.

FRERE, W. H. See p. 48.

KENNEDY, W. M.: *Life of Parker* (1908).

MAKOWER, F. See p. 48.

MEYER, A. O.: *England und die katholische Kirche unter Elisabeth und den Stuarts,* vol. i. (Rome, 1911). Translated by R. McKee (1916). Vol. i. deals only with Elizabeth's reign; vol. ii. is not yet published.

NEAL, D. See p. 48.

NOTESTEIN, W.: *History of Witchcraft in England from 1558 to 1718* (1911). This shows the extent of the Privy Council's interference in witchcraft cases.

PARKER, MATTHEW: *Correspondence.* See p. 48.

PEEL, A. See p. 48.

PIERCE, W. See p. 48.

POLLARD, A. F.: *Thomas Cranmer* (1904).

POLLEN, J. H.: *The English Catholics in the Reign of Queen Elizabeth.* A study of their politics, civil life, and government, 1558–1580 (1920).

Strype, J.: *Works.*   See p. 35.

Usher, R. G.: *The Reconstruction of the English Church* (2 vols., 1910).   *The Rise and Fall of the High Commission* (1913).   These two works indicate the relations of the Privy Council to the High Commission; the second has an excellent bibliography.

APPENDIX XV

A list of MSS. and printed books that are valuable for the history of the Star Chamber (see also Appendix VII.).

Accounts for Star Chamber Dinners—Scofield, C. L.: *Accounts of Star Chamber Dinners*, 1593. *A.H.R.*, vol. v., pp. 83-95 (October, 1899).   This prints the Dinner accounts in B.M. Add. MS. 32117D *in extenso,* and discusses the whole subject for the sixteenth century.   The " Account Book of the diet of the Council " for 15 and 16 Henry VIII. is summarised in *Letters and Papers,* vol. iv., Pt. I., No. 1097.   There are five more volumes of this series (29-37 Henry VIII.) among the Exchequer Accounts (bundle 96, Nos. 27-31), and there are five volumes of the expenses of the diet of the Star Chamber (Henry VIII. to Charles I.) in the Exchequer of Receipt Misc. 337-341 (see *P.R.O. List, No.* 35, p. 85).   There were also nine diet books of the Council (1519–1635) among the Alfred Morrison MSS. (*Hist. MSS. Com.,* 9th *Rep., App., Pt. II.,* p. 413; this collection is now dispersed), and there was a book of the charges for the Privy Council's diet in the Star Chamber from April 13 to May 8, 1638, among the MSS. of J. Eliot Hodgkin (*Hist. MSS. Com.,* 15th *Rep., App. II.,* p. 295).   In the British Museum there are accounts for the Council's diet for 1509 and later years (Lansd. MS. 1, Arts. 44, 49), for 1545–1551 (Add. MS. 38134), for several years of Henry VIII.'s reign (Lansd. MS. 69, Art. 6), for 1588–1589 (Lansd. MSS.

58, Art. 60; 59, Art. 41), for 1591 (Lansd. MS. 69, Art. 3), and for 1593 (Add. MS. 32117D); there are considerations of the need of reducing these expenses noted in the *Hist. MSS. Com., 3rd Rep., App.*, p. 53, and *4th Rep., App.*, pp. 277-278.

BRADFORD, G.: *Proceedings in the Court of the Star Chamber in the reigns of Henry VII. and Henry VIII.* Somerset Record Soc. (1911). There is quite a good introduction.

BROWN, W.: *Yorkshire Star Chamber Proceedings.* Yorkshire Archæological Soc. Record Series, vols. xli., xlv. (1909, 1911). The second volume is edited by H. B. McCall. These proceedings are selected from between the years 1485 and 1544.

BRUCE, J.: *History of the Star Chamber. Archæologia,* vol. xxv., pp. 342-393 (1834). This gives quite a good account of the Star Chamber procedure based on Hudson.

CARTER, A. T.: *Council and Star Chamber. Law Quarterly Review,* vol. xviii., p. 247 (July, 1902).

CHENEY, E. P. See p. 53.

GARDINER, S. R.: *Reports of Cases in the Courts of Star Chamber and High Commission.* Camden Soc., New Ser., No. 39 (1886). The Star Chamber cases run from Easter term, 1631 to Trinity term, 1632.

GARDINER, S. R.: *Documents relating to the Proceedings against William Prynne in 1634 and 1637.* Camden Soc., New Ser., No. 18 (1877).

GIUSEPPI, M. S.: See p. 54.

HOLDSWORTH, W. S.: *A History of English Law* (7 vols.; only 3 vols. so far published, 1921–1923). Vol. i. contains a rather brief account of the Star Chamber (pp. 477–525); vol. v. promises to be more valuable.

LEADAM, I. S.: See pp. 53, 54. There was quite an interesting article based on Leadam's book in the *Edinburgh Review,* vol. ccxv., p. 318 (1912).

List of Proceedings in the Court of Star Chamber. See p. 54.

POLLARD, A. F.: See p. 53.

SCOFIELD, C. L.   See p. 53.

STEWART-BROWN, R.: *Lancashire and Cheshire Cases in the Court of Star Chamber*, vol. i.   Record Society for the publication of Original Documents relating to Lancashire and Cheshire, vol. lxxi. (1916).   These range between 1485 and 1547.

TANNER, J. R.: *Tudor Constitutional Documents* (1922).

WHITE, E. F.: " The Jurisdiction of the Privy Council under the Tudors."   This unprinted thesis (for the London M.A.) contains a good deal on the Star Chamber in the sixteenth century.

WINFIELD, P. H.: *The History of Conspiracy and Abuse of Legal Procedure* (1921).   This says something of Star Chamber jurisdiction in these matters.